Matilda Penrose Fry

**Historic Memories and Other Poems**

Matilda Penrose Fry

**Historic Memories and Other Poems**

ISBN/EAN: 9783337006570

Printed in Europe, USA, Canada, Australia, Japan

Cover: Foto ©Thomas Meinert / pixelio.de

More available books at **www.hansebooks.com**

# HISTORIC MEMORIES

### AND

# OTHER POEMS.

BY

MATILDA FRY.

> Onward still, and still for ever,
> Down the swiftly gliding river;
> On, the silent steersman steering,
> Onward to the unseen veering;
> Naught is still but the tideless sea
> Which girdles round eternity.

*Not Published.*

LONDON.
1890.

# HISTORIC MEMORIES

AND

# OTHER POEMS.

BY

MATILDA FRY.

> Onward still, and still for ever,
> Down the swiftly gliding river;
> On, the silent steersman steering,
> Onward to the unseen veering;
> Naught is still but the tideless sea
> Which girdles round eternity.

*Not Published.*

LONDON.
1890.

THE FOLLOWING POEMS

ARE PRINTED BY

HER CHILDREN,

IN EVER AFFECTIONATE MEMORY

OF THEIR

BELOVED AND GIFTED MOTHER.

MATILDA FRY was the wife of FRANCIS FRY, of Bristol, whom she survived two years. She died 26th October, 1888, in her eightieth year.

Her poems were not intended for publication, nor were they finally revised by her.

# Contents.

|  | PAGE. |
|---|---|
| ALIANORE ... | 184 |
| AN ETRUSCAN TOMB | 23 |
| AND THERE ARE TIMES ... | 78 |
| ATTIL | 28 |
| BIND THE NIGHT SHADE | 121 |
| BOABDIL'S FAREWELL | 139 |
| CALCUTTA, 1765 ... | 93 |
| CRUSADER, THE ... | 95 |
| DEPARTURE, THE | 144 |
| DESERT PATH, THE | 75 |
| DOMINE QUO VADIS | 111 |
| DREAM, A | 31 |
| EL AIDEN | 123 |
| ETRUSCAN WARRIOR'S TOMB, THE | 57 |
| FALLING LEAVES REFLECTED ON THE WATER ... | 60 |
| FANCY | 71 |
| FAREWELL | 85 |
| FEAR NOT | 138 |
| FEVER | 73 |
| GERTRUDE S——N | 30 |
| GOTH IN ROME, THE | 127 |

|  | PAGE. |
|---|---|
| Go to the Rising Sun—Mine is at its Setting | 20 |
| Ida | 153 |
| Illness | 62 |
| In Memoriam | 63 |
| Iona | 191 |
| I would not have Thee Sorrow | 89 |
| Labarum, The | 46 |
| Last Sleep, The | 135 |
| Lepanto | 52 |
| Marius in Carthage | 83 |
| Martyr's Grave, The | 17 |
| Missal, The | 235 |
| Night in Granada, 1492 | 218 |
| On a Globe of Gold Fishes in a Sick Room | 237 |
| On the Ruins of Llanthony Abbey | 175 |
| Patrician Funeral | 42 |
| Paul of Tarsus | 1 |
| Remember Thee | 65 |
| Roderigo Ponce de Leon | 209 |
| Sickness | 151 |
| Siste Viator | 114 |
| Simplon, The | 90 |
| Sleeper, The | 81 |
| Stamboul | 68 |

|  | PAGE. |
|---|---|
| SUNRISE IN THE ALPS | 26 |
| "THE ROOM OF REST" | 119 |
| THOUGHT | 86 |
| THY NAME HATH PASSED | 117 |
| TINTERN ABBEY | 79 |
| TRIBUTE OF FLOWERS, THE | 130 |
| VALLEY OF SEPULCHRES—PALMYRA | 116 |
| WEEP NOT | 125 |
| WRITTEN NEAR LYONS | 88 |
| ZENOBIA | 33 |

## SONGS OF HOME.

| | |
|---|---|
| TO F. F. | 239 |
| TO S. M. F. | 242 |
| TO F. J. F. | 243 |
| TO T. F. | 246 |
| TO P. A. F. | 248 |
| TO W. G. F. | 250 |
| TO J. D. F. | 252 |
| TO C. P. F. | 254 |
| TO C. P. F. | 256 |

# PAUL OF TARSUS.

Where still Osiris, Isis, seem to brood,
And proud old Nile yet pours his wondrous flood;
That land of mystery, where elder time
Sits on his throne, dark, silent and sublime:
   From the fair City whose vast harbour holds
The ships of nations in its billowy folds;
Where the tall Pharos sheds its golden light,
Like hope in sorrow, o'er the wing of night,
Guiding the Tyrian galleys fast and free,
Far o'er the waters of a tideless sea;
Where treasures of the farthest earth were piled,
Wealth gaily grew, and radiant plenty smiled;
Whose gates of marble, graven pillars high,
And huge square towers in massive splendour lie;
Where Science dwells, and Soter's name shall live
Long as the past has any light to give.

From this proud mart, with canvas to the breeze,
Bounds the good ship, fast o'er the billowy seas:
Quick fades the City from the seaman's view,
Nor aught is seen save sea, and heaven of blue;
With fav'ring gales the bark wears bravely on
O'er the glad waves, till Myra's port is won;
But thence rough Boreas rides upon the blast,
And waves run high, and skies are overcast,
'Gainst winds and waves the ship makes tardy way
Breasting the billows to Fair Haven's bay.

. . . . .

Had the brave leader of Augustus' band
Pondered the words of one from Judah's land,
Paul—who for Israel's hope in fetters lay,
Scathless that good ship might have plough'd her way,
In harbour fair have borne the bitter blast,
With folded sails, till wintry winds were past;
Nor needed to have flung her anchors o'er,
Spite of the wild waves, and the tempest's roar.
Yet bravely has she with those wild waves striven,
'Till shivering planks and creaking spars are riven;
The giant seas lash o'er the crashing deck,
The ship's aground, black waves engulf the wreck.
" Plunge in the waters—breast the angry flood,
Seize floating spars, the timber yet is good,
Strain every nerve—the shore is nigh at hand:"

Such the deep voice of Julius to his band;
The huge waves yawn—the foaming surf beats high,
While human hearts breasting the billows lie,
And angry rocks resist the ceaseless roar,
Crested with foam that cannot find a shore.

Dire was the combat, till her sullen brow
Night hides, and morn reveals the scene below:
Haggard and worn those human shapes appear,
But Paul's stay'd heart throbs not with nature's fear;
For once in holy vision of the night
An angel came in panoply of light,
By the apostle stood, and bade him cheer,
His life was safe, for he must yet appear
At Cæsar's throne,—and for his sake were spared
The beating hearts of those that with him fared.

. . . . . .

Again to sea! spring hovers o'er the deep,
Bursts glorious nature from her wintry sleep:
Again to sea—the Nile boat hoists her sail,
And spreads her canvas to the southern gale;
The courteous Roman and his willing crew,
Paul and his friends, their seaward course renew;
The swart Egyptian longs to reach his home,
The Hebrews feel that they must yet see Rome.
O'er those calm waters where no storm-cloud flings

A sombre shadow from its dusky wings;
But rainbow hues pour soft and dreamy rays,
O'er the smooth wave that with the sunbeam plays;
Yes, all looks fraught with beauty and with bliss,
Round thy glad shores bright gay Neapolis;
So clear and brilliant the fond heart might deem,
All was the gorgeous tissue of a dream.
Calm o'er the expanse glides the vessel on
From the dim Nile—the wished-for harbour won.

Proudly the triremes float upon the bay,
Their white sails flashing in morn's sunny ray;
Helmet and cuirass glitter in the light,
Fresh from repose on the dusk wing of night;
The blue wave washes Puteoli's steep,
Where the grey mole invades the briny deep;
Whose loving waters gladly mirror back
The Pharos' rays, like Dian's gleamy track.
With even stroke fast plies the willing oar,
While its soft splash with music greets the shore;
And the bright earth arrayed in morning glee,
Dips its green margin in an azure sea;
Light gilds the ripple of each crested wave
Which those low shores now gently breaking lave;
Trails the wild vine o'er every jutting steep,
And crystal streams o'er flashing pebbles leap;

Music floats sighing through the dreamy trees,
And orange groves waft sweetness on the breeze,
While Parian shrines through the dark olives green,
Lend a last touch to the enchanting scene:
And o'er this wealth of beauty rising high
Vesuvius lifts his proud head to the sky,
Clad in a robe of ever varying hue,
Woven of roseate mists, and morning dew.

Where Claudian arches spread along the plain,
And nature laughs in her own gay domain;
Where Volscian hills rise dimly on the view,
Rich in the light Rome's early memories threw;
Where the clear Liris gently winding flows
In silver light, soft murmuring as it goes;
Where the dark forest lives along the plain,
And the rich fields foretell the golden grain;
Where Pontine marshes sickly vapours shed
Dank baneful dews upon the wanderer's head:
There Appius Claudius wrote upon the soil
His name in letters squared by Roman toil;
On that old road, whose broad stones wore no trace
Of time or change, in centuries' rapid race:
The path of ages, where Rome's mightiest trod
From the proud city to the azure flood:
There—Paul of Tarsus, mightier far than all

Passed with firm heart to Cæsar's judgment hall;
While o'er the pensive features of his face,
Fell the soft shadow of a heavenly grace;
And hope and gladness dewy freshness threw
Over his spirit, when the loved and true,
Earnest companions in that holy faith,
The Christian's sunshine, and his joy in death,
Met him—where Appii Forum marks the plain,
And Alba's hills rejoice in their domain:
Where in the pomp of human love and pride,
Homes of the dead stand thick on either side;
Where the sad cypress lifts its head on high,
Bathed in the radiance of a Roman sky,
And breathes the hoary spirit of the past,
While slumbering echoes waken to the blast;
As memory lifts the veil so folded o'er
The things and thoughts which were and are no more.

Rome's mighty pulse is felt,—the tide of life,
Its summer hues, its wintry look of strife;
Gladness and gloom, the freedman and the slave,
The great and gifted, timid hearts and brave,
Foreign and native, all now pour along,
And swell the murmurs of the morning throng:
Horsemen and foot, the noble and the base,
All onward move in life's uncertain race;

A passing look to the centurion band,
A question asked, perhaps a waving hand,
And all move on, while Paul with purpose high
And steadfast faith, is willing e'en to die.

On—through the suburbs spreading far and wide,
Dotted with villas in their marble pride,
Nestled in gardens, couched in shady groves,
On, with firm step the brave centurion moves:
Behind the prisoners—with sad weary march,
And downcast eyes through stern Capena's arch,
Beneath whose span what hosts have passed along
Life's varied tide, a countless motley throng!

The city gained—the hills their shadows cast,
The Cœlian, Aventine, are quickly past;
The Via Sacra to the Forum leads
Where dwells the spirit of Rome's mighty deeds;
Where Genius gilds with its undying light,
And gorgeous buildings almost dim the sight;
Nigh where Apollo's temple, Cæsar's home,
Lend still more spendour to Imperial Rome.
Here Julius halts, and instant his sad band
Pass from his charge, and now another hand
Fastens with courteous haste the Apostle's chain,
For guarded straitly he must yet remain.—

And years pass on, still Paul unwearied strove
To burst the chains that Pagan darkness wove;
From the pure fountain healing virtue shed,
And balm and gladness o'er the sorrowing spread;
Still ever fanning the Redeeming light,
Close by those fanes where brooded thickest night.

Now comes the moment of the Saint's appeal,
His cause he pleads before a heart of steel;
Pleads before Nero, whose dark sin-dyed face,
Seems as though reft of every human grace;
At Cæsar's seat, in Cæsar's judgment hall,—
That stern array might human heart appal;
But Paul of Tarsus fears no tyrant's nod,
His hope is sure, his faith is in his God.
Clad in the Christian's panoply, his form
Calmly awaits the issue of the storm;
No special pleading for a moment bowed
That fragile frame before the accusing crowd;
But with calm voice, when once allowed to speak
States he the cause, which made all others weak.
The hours wear on, the busy tongues are still,
All wait, expecting gloomy Nero's will;
A pause intense, then Cæsar's loud decree
Fills the wide hall, "the Christian—Paul is free."
His fetters burst, how glowed that noble breast!

Deep Christian feelings thronged to be expressed;
His Roman converts, children of his chains,
Must he them leave where Pagan darkness reigns?
Elsewhere to seek the weary, rouse their faith,
Ere round his head are wrapp'd the shades of death!
Onward for Christ then! first through Grecia's land,
That sunny clime, by soft sea breezes fann'd:
The glad East then, where Asia's churches lay,
To cheer their spirits ere he pass'd away.
Thence to far Spain, the cherished hope of years,
With earnest toil and many prayers and tears;
Hoping the warfare over, to remain
Where the fair city rises on the plain,
Nicopolis, where victory's eagles spread
Their regal plumes around Augustus' head;
Memorial proud of Actium's fearful fray,
When the triumvir's star fast paled away,
And Egypt's galleys faded from the view,
As o'er their prows fear on white feather flew,
And young Octavius placed upon his brow
Rome's gorgeous crown, a perished glory now.

And yet while winter mantles o'er the plain,
In those bright climes which seldom own his reign,
Paul to Nicopolis the message bears,
Love to the lost, and dries the sinner's tears;

Points to the light which shines beyond the tomb,
The Christian's hope in life's most dreary gloom;
With earnest heart, ere yet his sands were run,
Glad to depart, his armour girded on.
While preaching peace, the vengeful Pagan came:
—Enough to know he bore his Saviour's name,
Enough to forge his chains and send to Rome,
Crossing the sea, now white with wintry foam.

Rome, half in ruins, rises from the fire;
Like fabled bird when its bright days expire,
Springs from its ashes, spreading its gay plume,
Fresh as when first it wore youth's sunny bloom;
So the proud city springs up from the flame
In marble guise, another, yet the same,
Whilst Nero's minions on the Christians pour
The gloom, the madness of that awful hour;
Pour every torture fiends could e'er devise
On those whose home lay far beyond the skies.
Aged and worn the Apostle's feet once more
Pass the fair city, tread the dungeon floor,
In the dark mansions of the cruel laid,
Where hope is not, and human joys must fade;
And now more hard the weary fetters press
On the weak frame in nature's heaviness,
And not as once—when day its light could shed,

From Heaven's own sky around his aged head;
Aerial hues give place to dungeon gloom
And dark portents, the shadows of the tomb.
Those old walls sleep, and give not back the groans,
The human anguish, that might rend the stones;
The Tullianum guards its secrets well,—
Dark horrors float around that dreadful cell,
But from its depths what soft deep sounds arise,
The voice of praise has reached Heaven's holy skies;
For glory shines through depths of heathen gloom,
And peace and joy pervade the living tomb.

Life's shadows lengthen, and time quickly wanes,
Paul's hours are numbered—burnished are his chains;
Not human friendship always 'bides the blast,
When wrong or sorrow their dark omens cast;
The world's applause, its bubbles, or its cares,
Lift up the mask which sometimes friendship wears,
Shewing the native colour of the ore
Reft of the guise, which once perchance it wore.
Demas, thy name not yet hath passed away,
Type of a form which still exists in clay;—
But Paul of Tarsus suffers not alone,
Luke, the beloved physician, still loves on;
Stands by his side in weariness and ill,
As stars in darkest nights look brighter still:

So friendship, which has borne the fire of wrong
More purely shines—the furnace makes it strong.

Pleads once again the Apostle for his right
Before his Judge, and stern array of might:
No man stands by him, all forsake his chains—
But what to him are men or mortal pains?
His Saviour's presence sheds a holy light,
And all earth pales, with heavenly joys in sight:
Boldly he argues for the Christian faith,
His joy in life, his holy hope in death;
And death, vibrating in the scale with time
Pauses awhile, and stays the deed of crime.

A little while,—the sword hangs by a hair;
And those last days, are oh! how doubly dear!
A little band of loving hearts are true;
And well the suffering Saint might prize the few
Whose voices on his dungeon darkness fell;—
They who face death, must needs love true and well.

 . . . . . .

Come Sleep—breathe heavy on those eyelids now;
Fan with soft wings, that worn and aching brow,
Melt the hard chains, make soft the dungeon floor,
And on that way worn heart dear memories pour:

Almost those pale lips wear a dreamy smile,
Life's last oblivion all his cares beguile;
And vanished thoughts again fleet quickly o'er,
The shivering chords, which soon will throb no more.

On Taurus' height day's dying radiance flings
Its sunset hues, and flies on golden wings;
In its huge rifts the weary shadows sleep,
Watched by the clouds, that dim heaven's azure deep:
On Galilee the ripples scarcely wake
A sigh,—to stir the calmness of its lake;
The dashing Cydnus rolls in gladness by;
Ilex and myrtle to its eddies sigh;
Heaven's balmy air bears joy upon its breath,
In that hushed heart there broods no thought of death!
O'er its calm pulse, the wings of memory shed
The fond deep thoughts by early fancies fed;
'Tis his last dream—and with a heavy sigh
St. Paul awakes—to death, and glory nigh!

A few short hours—and human woe will be
Lost,—as earth's mists before the sunbeams flee.
Say, did Timotheus on that spirit pour
His wealth of heart on life's fast fading hour?
—Did the disciple on love's earnest wing
The last dear solace to his master bring?

—With low clear tones, on that fast closing ear
Pour the dear words, that Paul still longed to hear?
—Of souls released from Satan's galling chain,
From Pagan bondage and sin's gloomy reign?
—But brief the moments,—for his hour was come;—
Another crime to glut Imperial Rome.

The hush of noon rests on the city now;
Alba's blue hills bask gaily in the glow;
And far Soracte lifts his head on high
Over the plains that sleep in gladness by;
Scarcely a shadow o'er Avernus creeps,
Or dims the azure of the waveless deeps;
The wide Campagna with its waste of flowers,
Laughs in its beauty at the passing hours:
Scarcely the green pine lends its grateful shade,
True in its depths, when brighter colours fade;
Wooing the breeze to give its soft caress,
Stolen from those scented flowers in summer dress
All seems so full of beauty and of light,—
Say is there room for one dark deed of night?

Yes! the Mamertine from its horrid deep
Gives up the heart whose pulses long for sleep;
No shadow rests upon his heavenly sky,
But through his Saviour, crown and victory:

Death is to him a radiance from the tomb,
And Angels wait, to waft his spirit home.

There is a sound of feet;—upon the ear
Falls the dull tread—it comes, more sharp and clear;
Now—all is still—Rome's iron soldiers wait,
Moveless as statues, at the dungeon gate.
Clanks a dull chain,—a care-worn face appears,—
Those deep set eyes, beyond the reach of tears,
Shine with clear rays, which are not of the earth;
The still pure light, that is of Heavenly birth:
His fetters loosen, and now straight proceed—
Of further speech Rome's veterans had no need:
The hills lend shadow, but nor sun, nor shade,
Is ought to him on whom the Cross is laid;
The Palatine, with memories crusted o'er,
All that earth holds, can win a thought no more.

On press the crowds, of every race and clime;
'Twas nought to him who now had done with time:
A laugh,—a jeer,—perhaps a heartfelt sigh,
And the unflinching troop still pass them by;
The Circus, Aventine, are quickly past;
The Ostian gate, Paul's earthly bourne,—at last—
Without the gate—the headsman lifts the sword,—
The soul is free—for ever with its Lord.

Near the grey tomb, whose shadow softly falls
With airy grace, beyond the Servian walls;
The noble pyramid which proudly keeps,
Its silent watch where the stern Roman sleeps;
There—the high pulses of that noble breast
With martyr zeal, have borne him to his rest!
Say, did those heaven-bent eyes a moment light
Upon that pile, ere closed in nature's night,
Soon to awake where saints and angels sing
The endless song to Heaven's eternal King?

## THE MARTYR'S GRAVE.

"The deep cold waters close o'er one;
"Another sheds a crimson river—
"No matter; either stream returns
"A life to the Eternal giver:
"Each tinges with a glorious dye
"The Martyr's robe of victory."
Prudentius.

HEAVEN'S vigil stars had lent their loving light,
No sound disturbed the stillness of the night;
For anguished wailings were wrapt up in grief,
And burning eyes had not the blest relief
Of dewy tears—the heart too highly wrought
Swathed itself deep in that one anxious thought.
To steal those dear remains by night away:—
Now wrap in scanty shroud that gory clay;
In trembling haste seek out some lonely path,
Nor trust thy treasure to the Roman's wrath;
Fast seek the sandy mine, and quickly turn
The sharp descent—far on, they dimly burn
A shaded lamp, hard by the Pagan urn:

The lab'rynth passage shall secure thee well,
Day's glimmering light can reach the holy cell;
A narrow shaft leads on to upper air;
With noiseless steps the lost, the loved one bear!
Some Christian brother will thy steps await:
Close by the olives bear thy precious freight,
Fear not those regions of decay and gloom,
Life changed with death—there make the martyr's tomb!

Quickly descend into the lower stage,
On the rude shrine there lies the holy page;
The cold dark chapel holds another dead;
Beware the crypts—the fitful lamp will shed
Its scanty rays, and serve to lead thee down;
List to the dirge for him who wears the crown!
—Love's echo, passing on from cave to cave
Bears broken hearts upon its billowy wave:
There rest, a bier is ready for thy dead,
And soon the solemn ritual will be said;
Then weep—the heart is honor'd by such tears,
Affection's jewels set for after years;
Join with low voice the martyr's holy hymn
Breathed forth from ashen lips, by torches dim;
Then take thy dead from off the hasty bier
And lay the loved one in the middle tier:

Scooped was that narrow cell but yesterday,
And now earth holds not heart of finer clay;
Caius shall carve his image on the stone;
Rest, weary one—Heaven has but claimed its own;
Let sacred symbol on his relics lie
Carved in quick haste,—his memory must not die!

The rite was o'er; and all was yet still night;
Gray darkness lent its mantle for the flight
From out the crypts, and as dawn softly stole
From its own heaven, like light upon the soul,
The weary Christian felt his life was there,
And grief was wrapt in the soft hue of prayer:
As one by one, light called the stars to heaven,
It seemed to shadow to his soul the riven,
The radiant spirits, who had gone before
To that bright region, whither he might soar
Through the Redeemer's name, and by His cross;
And bowed in heart he felt all else was dross.

Temple and column stood in high relief
'Gainst the blue sky, which seemed to feel his grief;
O'er his hushed heart there stole a holy calm;
Faith, from her azure wings, dropp'd healing balm;
His weary eye glanced not on fanes or towers,
Nor rested e'en on those loved cypress bowers;

But like a Shade, silent he pass'd away,
While slumbering Rome in morning splendour lay,
And reached the Christian's shrine, where morning prayer
Was offer'd up—and laid his burden there.


## "GO TO THE RISING SUN—MINE IS AT ITS SETTING."

The air was laden with sighs of gloom,
    A monarch was passing to rest;
On an iv'ry couch in a gorgeous room,—
    Lit with rays from the golden west.

Rays from the sun on throne of even,
    Shed a mellow and waning light;
Farewell beams of the purple heaven
    Faintly fell on the monarch's sight;

And perfumes floated on Indian wings,
    And rich vases of crystal threw
Rays, which the beautiful Iris brings,
    When she spans heaven's arch of blue;

And poised she lay on her zephyr wings,
    Life's perishing chords to sever;
Bearing the curtain which darkness flings
    'Twixt time—and the great For-ever.

. . . . . .

Pure sparkling gems and cups of amber,
    Brass from Corinth, cameos rare,
And antique carvings grace the chamber,
    While Phidias lives in marble there.

On cedar stands lie Murrhine vases,
    Bright glass of Egypt, ruby red;
But what e'en thrones—to him who pauses
    From life's vain glitter on that bed?

On him gently place the covering,
    Tyrian purple, fold on fold;
O'er him scented plumes are hovering
    Gay Argus' feathers laced with gold.

An Antonine is passing over
    To the dim land of shadows now!
Rome's mighty Cæsar! dares death hover
    O'er that most pale and regal brow?

The spirit still is clear and gifted,
    And waits the Tribune for his will;
The purpose that mild eye hath sifted—
    The soul is Antoninus' still!

Com'st thou to see an emperor dying?
    Behold those red gates in the west,
Through their bright portals light is flying,
    The sun fulfils his high behest:

That sun will yet return in glory,
    And Rome, proud Rome, will look the same;
And day will write its golden story
    Upon the site so dear to fame.

But I go where the darkness gathers,
    Where monarchs can no favours shed,
On—to the pale shades of my fathers,
    To the dim land that holds the dead.

Now sets my Star—and sets for ever,
    The rising sun must warm thy brow;
Go thou to him whose golden quiver
    Holds all imperial favours now.

The shadows lengthen on life's dial,—
    Faint and still fainter comes each breath;
The great, the good, has pass'd time's trial,
    And Hades opes her gates to Death.

## AN ETRUSCAN TOMB.

Descend those steps, and breathlessly await
The dark unfoldings of that narrow gate;
The gray sepulchral stone is leaning still
Against the rock, upon the sloping hill;
Pass the dark portal of that ancient tomb;
With solemn step slow pace its stilly gloom;
Gaze on the door post cold gray travertine,
With letters old as the Etruscan line;
Oh! could those strange dark characters be told,
So sharply graven, what would they unfold?

Daylight belongs not to that far off hour;
Light ye the torches! let them softly pour

Rays on the roof so rich in vaulted pride;
Then on the silent chambers at the side
Of the arched tomb; and cast thine eager eyes,
At the end vault sown thick with mysteries:
On seven fair coffers, with their carvings rare,
Lie the cold guardians of the mansion drear:
Each on his stony bier—low resting now
With jewel'd neck and chaplet on the brow,
And cup in hand, as if to-day had been
The gay embodiment of some bright scene;
Medusa guarding,—while in dreamless rest
This home of ages holds each stony guest.
At either end with snakes and blazing torch,
A stern winged Fury guards death's solemn porch,
With eyes upturned, as if for gleams of light,
Yet ever brooding on a dawnless night.
Gaze on the ceiling of that inner room,
Look at the Gorgon head in its still gloom;
Hewn in the solid rock, those glaring eyes
Gleam forth grim horrors as they upward rise;
With snakes thick knotted round that dusky head
And open mouth—you feel with shivering dread,
Whispers and hisses soon must change the air,
And pale with dread the sickly torches glare.
Upon a shield, bedight with scale on scale,
Apollo's head lies girt with laurel mail.

With bird and scimetar,—we dimly know
The symbol language these spake long ago.
Gone are the Demons from their place of guard,
One dreamy wing out-spread alone keeps ward;
But crested snakes still dart with arrowy force
Their subtle tongues as if to guard the corse;
The Furies emblem; but the words below
Those time-worn letters are too faint to show.
Gone are the offerings of love and pride;—
Gorgons and serpents, and owls staring wide
Haunt the dim gloom: all else has pass'd away,
Wrapt in the shadows of Time's morning gray;
But the strange letters linger on, and show
To living hearts that dust still lies below.
And thought lay hushed beneath the mighty power
The spell-bound interest of that thrilling hour,
When the dim Past, as with a mighty wave,
Rolled itself back from the Etruscan's grave.

## SUNRISE IN THE ALPS.

O'er all the vale hung morning's mist, between
The gazing eye and that most lovely scene:
Slowly it rose, unveiling by degrees
The happy homestead girt by Alpine trees,
The rushing river and the glacier gray,
Looking almost as in its first array,
When the Almighty vouched his wondrous plan
Of grace and mercy to his creature, man.
High and still higher, flies the feathery cloud;
Alp after Alp leaps glorious from its shroud,
Till the last peak lies throned against the sky,
In all the might of mountain majesty.
On its white crest robed in eternal snow,
See Phœbus' rays in morning's matchless glow;
Onward his coursers speed and still ascend,
And in one glow of beauty all things blend.
The Alpine peaks reflect his glittering rays,
The glacier cold his look of love repays;
The dark green pines, like emeralds stud the snow,
The dashing stream gives back the heavenly glow;

The smiling chalets deck the mountain slope,
And happy homesteads, rich in health and hope:
The wayworn traveller, and the sad in heart,
If such in scene like this can have a part,
All feel the influence of the risen day,
And glad or gloomy bend the knee to pray;
The chapel bell resounds along the steep,
And Switzer's horn, with tone so clear and deep;
The hum of voices gathers through the vale;
The scent of opening flowers perfumes the gale,
Their dewy petals hail the god of day,
And in their silent beauty bless his ray,
Whose heavenly course has steeped all things in light
And paled the stars that lit the brow of night;
Flinging o'er wakened life ethereal dress,
Morn—in her pride, and prime, and loveliness!

## ATTIL.

Thou art gone from the humming birds,
   From the bright azalea's bloom,
From the sound of love's balmy words,
   To the stillness of the tomb.

From the butterfly on azure wings
   In its beauty floating by;
From the pale stars whose lustre flings
   Mute glory o'er thy native sky.

Thou hast gone from thy sunlit isle,
   Begirt by that far off sea;
And the fond looks that met thy smile
   Will be dark—with grief for thee.

For the loss of the early dead—
   For the sweet young blossom riven;
From the stem where its sweets were shed
   To bloom in the light of Heaven.

And calm death stole so softly by,
    Thine ear scarcely caught his tread;
A sigh—a pause—a deeper sigh—
    And bowed was thy lovely head.

But full soon came the glazing eye;—
    And the sad and moveless air
Bore the weight of a parting sigh,
    And death brooded darkly there.

Over thy graceful form no more
    The feathery palm shall wave;
Nor tropic flowers in sorrow pour
    Sweet incense o'er early grave:

But England's cloudy sky shall weep
    Tear drops that thou can'st not see;
And memory shall love's vigil keep,
    Attil,—in mindfulness of thee.

Thus in sadness we lay thee down
    To rest 'neath our emerald sod:
And for ever to wear thy crown
    In the paradise of God.

### GERTRUDE S———N.

Look again at that bright being,
    While the earliest dew of life
Shines with its pale rays upon her;
    In her joyous beauty rife.

See the light well-nigh ethereal,
    Beaming through those starry eyes;
Their radiant pupils always on you,
    Always—with a glad surprise.

And question why you gaze upon her?
    With such loving look—so slow
To move your eyes from her fair features,
    From her silken tresses glow.

Her pale cheek looks not any redder,
    Her eyes still give their violet light,
Her still lips part not, yet she asks you,
    Why seems she ever in your sight?

Fold a soft white robe upon her,
   'Twill make her lovely face more fair,
And her lashes look still darker
   In the waves of her golden hair.

Fling a blue veil gently o'er her,
   Well it shades her placid brow:
And let the dreamy orbs beneath it
   Ever shine on us as now.

## A DREAM.

—And sleep with her calm stilly step past by,
And breathed on those eyelids a heavy sigh;
And lit up the lamp of a perished hour,
In all its beauty and all its power;
And the hopes of to-day and hues that are
Lay folded up deep, 'neath the things that were;
Till hearts that were riven again are one,
As memory basks in a day long gone:
And the voice that for years had not been heard
Floated sweeter than song of the summer bird;

And the loving looks, which must never beam,
Came true o'er the heart in that golden dream;
As the honied accents of love and truth
Gushed warm from the lips as in early youth;
For the soft warm colour of other days
Had wrapt up old Time in its amber rays:
Forgotten the grave, as in long review
Came one by one, the loved vanished and true:
The spells of the sleeper had banished the shroud
And broken the cerement, as light breaks the cloud;
The story of life rushed again o'er the heart,
And the eyes looked as bright as still they had part
In the hours now floating away on time's wing,
As if death had not been, and life held no sting;
But rushed in the daylight, and faded away
The beautiful forms to their houses of clay.
The dreaming was over, and life came between
The quick beating pulse, and the life that had been;
For a moment—less real the outward—and then
The Present took up her bright sceptre again.

## ZENOBIA.

Her Arab waits—the Queen will ride to-day,
Proud of his freight, that Beni Hassan gray—
Fleet as an arrow, gentle as a sigh,
With almost language in his drooping eye,
He paws the ground, and, snorting for the chase,
Tosses his silky mane, and waits the race.

She comes; Zenobia, in her beauty rare,
With ostrich plumes, inwoven in her hair
Black as the raven's wing, with softened rays
Of feathery light, that in its darkness plays;
A band of gold supports the ebon tress,
Bound up in beauty for the wilderness;
Her bright cheek looks as if the desert air
Had fanned itself into a soft home there,
And kissed those eyes, whose depths of starry light,
So softly calm, so beautifully bright,
Gladdened the hearts of all within her sway
Queen of the East, the Cynosure of day.

" Speed for the desert, let my train come on,
" Princes! we slack not till the spoil is won;
" The lion's roar full soon may greet our ear;
" Let him stay back,—who knows the hue of fear.
" The imperial purple clothes my sons to-day,
" Quick let them doff it for the desert fray!"
So spake that noble heart, and with a bound
Her Arab courser lightly touched the ground:
Snuffing the desert air, he sped away,
Till distance wrapped Palmyra in its gray;
Nor flagged that brilliant staff, till set of sun
With reddened rays, pronounced the labour done.

And night, calm glorious night, came on;
From out its starry depths the pale moon shone,
Lighting with silver rays that sandy sea.
Coldly sublime in its immensity;
Shedding its loving looks on that fair isle,
Whose sunny verdure made the desert smile;
On marble columns, glancing far and wide;—
Stately Palmyra! in thine hour of pride
Did no dark dream, or hovering genius say,
That proud and glittering scene should pass away?
That fanes and towers, and that most gorgeous pile,
Should sleep in ruins on the desert isle;
That stately palms, so rich in sorrowing grace,

From age to age, should mark their resting place;
And shiver'd columns in their marble grief,
And wrecks of temples in still blue relief,
'Gainst heaven's clear sky, and on that sandy sea,
Be all that Time's rough wave should spare of thee?

Gone are the stirring days of high emprise,
And hours of study, when those earnest eyes
Drank deep of Homer, and that queenly brow
Leant in wrapt silence to the earnest flow
Of truths sublime, when wise Longinus spake,
And mind, and eye, and ear, were all awake;
The daring deeds, the trophies of the war,
The Empress worship which she drew from far,
Are gone, as shadows on Time's dial flee;—
Thou changing earth, can aught abide on thee?

Brave Odenathus wields no sceptre now,
The cares of empire weigh not on his brow,
The gorgeous dreams which floated through his breast
In his cold heart for ever are at rest;
No more exulting shall his troops press on,
Victorious to the gates of Ctesiphon;
The fell assassin laid the mighty low;
A shade—a dream, is Odenathus now;
Yet still Zenobia holds her mighty state,

Her sons grew round her and with hearts elate,
A loving people owned the gentle hand,
Which spread such blessings on their sunny land;
Ere from the West drew on that boding cloud,
So soon to wrap a nation in its shroud:
Ere fierce Aurelian saw the prize from far,
And loosed his eagles for the desert war.

Then came the hours of darkness and of gloom,
The Fates had woven in their fearful loom:
In vain Zenobia sought to stem the tide,
Or stay the victor in his hour of pride;
Bravely she met the Roman on his way,
Let Antioch witness to that dreadful day!
Emesa too, but the stern strife was vain—
Mournful, she sought her palmy home again;
Her mighty hosts had quickly past away,
Like snows on Taurus 'neath the solar ray;
Gone like a meteor is her regal state,
The legions press—Aurelian's at the gate.
Like the wild tiger crouching for the spring,
Or vulture, poised on broad expecting wing,
The conqueror watched; Palmyra in his grasp,
Woe to thee, Tadmor, held in Rome's stern clasp!

Night came,—all hope had with the daylight died,

Zenobia, flying, sought Euphrates' side;
A bark lay floating on its moonlit breast,
So cold and bright, it almost promised rest;
The silver tide gave back the soft calm gaze,
Which lit its waters with those glancing rays;
With lightning speed her hopes are on the river,
A moment more, and they are lost for ever;
For eagle eyes had tracked her rapid flight
Through gleam and shadow on that fearful night;
The light troop grimly by the river's side
Drew weary rein, elate with victors' pride;
In woe majestic the proud Queen arose,
Sorrow but made her nobler, and her foes
A moment paused, awed by the stately mien,
The quiet grandeur of Palmyra's Queen.

One dewy glance she gave her own loved stream,
Now for the city of life's brilliant dream;
Faded, as fade the purple hues of even,
When night sends back day's sapphire robe to heaven;
Not with exulting steps she hied her home,
But, worn and weary, swathed in deepest gloom:
Home! her own Tadmor, memory's scorching breath
Dries up her heart, and makes her sigh for death;
But no! a suppliant to triumphant Rome,
Aurelian's lips must first pronounce her doom.

Draw we the curtain o'er that gloomy hour,
When that high heart for once forgot its power:
When in the weakness of that weary frame
Herself excused—she marred Longinus' name,
The great, the gifted—ere the victor gave
His fame to ages, to himself, a grave.
Oh! let the memory of her nobler time
Cast a thick veil upon that hour of crime,
And pity shed its lovely radiance o'er
The desert's gem, alas! to shine no more;
Reserved to grace Aurelian's triumph now,
Before his car to march with gloomy brow
From early morn, till night drew on her crown
And veil of stars, in fadeless lustre strown,
To see Rome's pageant, and to feel the power
Of her stern victor in his glorious hour;
Oh! let soft night weigh down with dewy sleep
Those weary eyes, which feel too sad to weep;
Let rosy morn upon her fresh dipt wing,
Some rays of comfort to the captive bring;
Let mercy triumph, though stern justice bow,
And glad Aurelian be all-gracious now.

With noiseless step through night's wide ebon gates
Dawn gently comes, and on the conqueror waits;
Instant he hails the sign, and all prepare

The fitting trophies for the great in war.
O'er his broad shoulders place, with fold on fold,
The purple robe full thickly dight with gold;
Then joyful pay the just and fitting rite
To Rome's high guardians who have ruled the fight;
Slowly move o'er the long triumphal way,
And strew bright flowers to greet the gladsome day;
Upon the altars fragrant incense spread,
While wreaths of smoke benignant vapours shed;
Let various music and the voice of song
With thrilling sound, the joyous notes prolong;
Round the gilt horns the fillets bravely bind,
With flowery garlands and green verdure twined;
Then bring the spoils, the varied wealth of war,
Till the broad pavement groans beneath each car;
While carved on wood is many a mighty name
For ever crushed, to give Aurelian fame.
Princes and rulers, and a motley throng
Of sorrowing captives, next the scene prolong,
Whose weary steps the Lictors urge to death,
Their cruel fasces decked with laurel wreath;
And one—oh! shame upon the human heart,
Insults the fallen with mock'ry's poisoned dart;
While music spreads its voice upon the air,
And golden crowns give back the sunny glare,
And onward march, in pomp of glittering white,

Rome's best and bravest in their togas dight.
Then slowly passing through the perfumed air,
Comes glittering on the Conqueror's ivory car.
Behold great Cæsar as he stands erect,
In purple mantle, with pure gold bedeck'd!
Round his high forehead, wind the conqueror's bays,
Jove-like, his face lights up with vermeil rays;
The golden ball hangs proudly from his neck.
To crush dark envy, and all malice check ;
One hand the laurel holds with nervous grasp,
The left the sceptre with its ivory clasp.
With proud arched neck the white steeds onward move
To the great temple of Rome's patron, Jove:
While the swart slave who bears the glittering crown
Behind the victor, tamely crouches down,
Yet ever whispers in Aurelian's ear,
Mortal thou art, hast thou no cause of fear?
Next, closely following Cæsar's gorgeous car,
March, laurel deck'd, the steel-clad ranks of war;
" Io Triumphes " shake the laughing hills,
And loud-tongued praise the cup of victory fills.
The Forum gained—the prisoners' hour is come,
To the Gemonium! all that war with Rome;
Halt!-- till the ebb of that ensanguined tide—
Till hearts are drained, and anguish opened wide.

Hope's rainbow rises o'er Zenobia's gloom,
And life is spared for happier hours to come;
Aurelian's hands the golden links untie—
It is enough, the weary captive's sigh
Wafts Tadmor's Queen to Tibur's broad domains,
And pity melts the Roman's galling chains;
The milk-white beasts now offer up to Jove,
From far Clitumnus where they wont to rove;
Thy jewell'd crown upon his altar lay,
And homeward Cæsar, bend thy victor way.

. . . . . .

Go to the Sibyl's Temple, where it keeps
Its watch of ages, on those craggy steeps;
Fair Tibur, where the foaming Anio smiles
In its wild course adown those steep defiles,
Where power, and wealth, and genius, higher still,
Bent earth's bright treasures to their sovereign will;
For there Zenobia breathed her sunset hours,
No regal thorns disturbed life's fading flowers.
And if, in memory of other days,
Her eyes dropt diamonds, rich in sorrow's rays,
Blame not the thoughts, which oft to Tadmor flew,
On heavy wings, in Time's long sad review;
Blame not the memories woven in the heart,
Gray sorrow's day-dreams which would not depart,

But o'er the fallen a softened halo shed,
Time's purple mists, with orient colours spread;—
Her brilliant hour, let history's tablets keep,
And spread fame's starry curtain o'er her sleep.


## PATRICIAN FUNERAL.

Give back, oh! give me back, the perished years,
When Caius stood, the pride of all his peers,
Hope of his house, till blighting sickness came,
And shook the mighty sinews of his frame;
Till death had laid him on his ivory bier;
Ah, woe is me, that he should slumber here!
As next of kin I closed his fading eye,
With a sad kiss inhaled the parting sigh,
Took off the ring, and once more breathed his name,
With a farewell to everything but fame.
The perfumed corse we clothed in costly dress,
And flowers were strewed in the heart's weariness:
On his dear form, the feet placed next the door,
The last sad time his shadow would pass o'er
The storied tracery of the marble floor.

Lay in the vestibule the noble dead,
And silent poppies gently o'er him spread;
Softly a vase of limpid water bring,
Mind thou it wells up from the purest spring;
Place Charon's money in the mouth, from whence
Once rushed the burning tide of eloquence;
Bring cypresses, those dark funereal trees,
Let them sigh softly to the wailing breeze,
Telling to all, what we too sadly know—
That Caius' house is now the house of woe.

By blazing torches we shall take thee forth
From the rich home, made richer by thy worth;
Foremost thy feet, and on the inlaid bier
Thy dearest friends and most distinguished near;
So shall we bear thee from thy home away,
Tyre's purple loom shall shroud the noble clay;
The solemn Lictors shall in black be drest,
With fasces down to guard thee to thy rest;
Before thy corse, thine image shall be borne,
Which long on mournful hearts shall yet be worn;
Ancestral shades, " Imagines " shall grace
The long procession to thy resting place,
And solemn music caught from the sad air,
Shall breathe its wailing notes upon thy bier,
With voices hired to sing thee to thy rest,

And one, sad mockery, in thy garments drest—
For oh, what madness to think aught could be,
E'en for a moment, made to look like thee!
Let kindred hearts now sadly follow on,
Clad in deep mourning, for their pride is gone.
Let the Patricians leave their gauds at home,
But all the freedmen may the cap put on;
The type of liberty they drew from thee,
And now all silence let the Atrium be.

March with slow movement—to the Forum go,
Halt at the Rostrum! say, can language show
Half what thou wast, or picture thee in life;
'Tis well, but all in vain the loving strife
To do thee worship, and the long array,
With mournful steps, must reach the Appian way.

Build high the pyre with costly wood and spice,
In altar shape, as if for sacrifice.—
Slowly the bier is raised, for Caius lies
Outstretched upon it, and once more his eyes
Have their lids opened, but alas! no light
Can pierce the shadow of that endless night;
Close them again, and let the long array
Move slowly round the cold and senseless clay,
To solemn music, while with hair unbound,

And eyes cast softly, sadly, on the ground ;
Let Roman matrons, each with cypress wreath
Chant the last requiem in the ear of death ;
Let him who touched the eyes, now light the pyre,
On the dead look not, while thy torches' fire
Spreads sudden blaze ;—must dust and ashes be
All that remains, thou gifted one, of thee ?
And ye who loved him, throw the sweet perfume
And costly spices ; while the flames consume
That form, which seemed too beautiful to die,
Proudly dilating with its spirit high !

The flames sink lower, feebler, fainter, yet
More and more fitful,—now the light is set :
Vermilion embers cast a lurid glare
Upon the hearts that beat in anguish there ;
Bring costly wine and pour upon the fire,—
With that fond act, how many hopes expire !

Darker, still darker, grows that cherished clay.—
And now in costly vase those ashes lay ;
In fitting tomb the precious relics place,
To rest in glory, with his gifted race ;
And in your inmost hearts be folded deep,
Soft thoughts of him, which never must know sleep ;
Thus bathed in memory's moonlight, he shall throw

Like a pale star, far rays to light your woe.
Now, thrice the priest shall lustral water shed
From laurel branch upon each drooping head;
Slowly pronounce the solemn parting word,
The " Ire licet;" how life's depths are stirred!
The last farewell from trembling lips has come,
And now the *cippus* marks thy honored tomb.


## THE LABARUM.


Silence lay brooding o'er that mighty host,
The calm, the moody, and the tempest toss'd:
All was as still, as if dark mighty death
Had paused a moment, and caught up their breath;
Night had unfolded her soft ebon wing,
Laden with stars of old Time's gathering.

The camp was hushed, but still young Caesar kept
Unslumbering vigil while the legions slept;
He felt that war was grimly gathering on,

And he must face it ere the prize be won;
'Gainst murmurings deep, and fears that found a
    breath,
He still resolved on victory or death;
With fearful odds against him, four to one,
He stood in majesty, but stood alone.

Day dawned, and all was duty in the camp,
With cuirass bracing, and the mighty tramp
Of armed heel, as girding up for war,
Like men who scented battle from afar;
But still with doubt and gloom upon the brow,
Rome's legions seldom looked as they looked now.

The moody general then invoked the power
Of the true God, in his most fearful hour,
If such there were, to grant him grace and might
With His right arm, in the unequal fight,
When looking heavenward as with an evil eye,
Full on the sunshine; oh, what mystery!—
He saw, with eyes dilated for the sight,
Over the sun a radiant cross of light,
And on it traced in characters of flame,
"Conquer by this!"—the emblem of His name;
Amazement seized him, and the portent ran
With lightning speed, along that glittering van.

Night's mantle fell, and the soft folds of sleep
Had wrapped young Cæsar in its mantle deep;
And like some noble image, calm he lay,
Clad as a warrior in his steel array.
O'er his chained eyelids stole an awful sight,
A glorious Being clothed in rays of light,
Bearing the sign which in the heaven had been
Over the sun, and by his cohorts seen;
And from his lips there fell the high command,
The Cross should be the standard of the land,
And he should conquer by the holy sign,
Which beamed in heaven, effulgent and divine.

Woke Constantine, and high command was given,
To frame the standard from its type in heaven;
And bright the Labarum in radiance rose
Young Cæsar's best defence against his foes;
A brilliant ensign, spear enwrapt with gold,
With rays so bright, the eyes could scarce behold;
The flag, o'erlaid with every brilliant gem
Which else might glitter on a diadem.
And at the top, with precious stones and gold
A radiant crown, with symbol bright, enrolled,
The monogram of that most precious Name—
The Grecian letters in their jewelled frame.
No more of murmuring or delay was there,

But stout hearts beating with the pulse of war,
And quickly passing from that mighty river
Which seemed to flow as it would flow for ever,
Left Gaul behind and bent their onward way
Where the proud Alps in unveiled grandeur lay.
Slowly they wound along the mountain height,
Their burnished mail gave back the morning light;
The sacred standard blazing like a star,
Now foremost graced the billowy ranks of war;
At length descending, where Segovia lowers
Across their path, with all its bristling towers;
But soon reduced, the victor marches on,
And dark Taurinum's battlements are won;
Verona too, grown rich in pride and power;—
All own its might, the standard rules the hour;
And the Flaminian yields an easy way
To the stern cohorts in their dread array.

Maxentius' front at Saxa Rubra lay,
Tiber's right bank held strong his other way;
His serried ranks like wave on wave came on,
But like the waves, they rose, and soon were gone;
In vain they fought where'er the bright sign led,
The brave Prætorians in long files lay dead.
The Tiber swallowed what the field had spared,
And dark Maxentius, long the hated, feared,

On the rent bridge his sullen bulk upreared
Above the crashing mass, and disappeared;
Gorged by the yellow Tiber, in its flood,
Not yellow now, but red with Roman blood

The seven-hilled City stands in dreamy sight,
Pale autumn's sun fast gilding it with light;
And glancing on the bucklers where the sign
Of the Cross rests, all conquering and divine:—
On o'er the Tiber, as the morn's young ray
Lights up the Sabine hills with vapoury play;
Broken the Milvian bridge, the troops must pass
Over the Campus Martius, whose soft grass
Is emerald, to the weary eye of war,
And path of triumph for the victor's car.
Its marble temples fascinate the sight,
Its shady groves soft veil the fervid light;
While tow'ring high o'er those of lesser fame
Augustus' pile still guards the Julian name;
Thence the freed eagle took its daring flight
Bearing the Emp'ror's genius from the sight.

Let all come forth in their most rich array,
To see the splendours of this gracious day;
Let the bright sun his orient splendour pour
With double gladness, 'tis great Cæsar's hour.

Let the bronze gates fly back, as morn's first light
Folds quickly up the dusky wing of night;
And acclamation, stirring the seven hills,
Rome, gorgeous Rome, with seven-fold glory fills.

Onward the Labarum, still onward flies,
See the Tarpeian, rich in memories rise;
Pass by the Circus, towards the Cœlian march,
And next advance to the triumphal arch.
The sacred way now claims the moving tide,
The conquering legions, in their pomp and pride;
And now—the Capitol—and on its height,
The saving standard sheds its dawning light;
The dark Mamertine's weary bonds are riven,
And hope and gladness to the captives given,
The Christian's faith dispels the night of gloom,
And all is sunshine in Imperial Rome.

## LEPANTO.

Safe the Moslem fleet at anchor
   On the deep blue waters lay;
Not a ripple on its surface
   Stirred the sapphire of the bay.

The turban'd host in dreamy silence
   Calmly watched the orient rays,
As they rose o'er sea and mountain
   Through the folds of purple haze;

Dashing sunbeams on the waters,
   Brilliant fields of waving light;
Ere Lepanto's awful slaughter
   Turned that radiant morn to night.

Moves at last the proud Armada
   Through those Grecian Isles of light;
Sailing onward calm and stately,
   Till the bright cross waved in sight.

Where Achelous gives its waters
  To the clear Ionian wave,
There the Moslem, fierce and haughty,
  Met a host as firm and brave.

Quickly formed the bristling crescents,
  Face to face along the sea;
Quickly came the battle order,
  And the flags wav'd high and free.

There Don John, the proud and gifted,
  Led his forces o'er the main;
A hundred sail obeyed his mandate
  From the mighty land of Spain.

Doria brought his dashing galleys,
  Genoa's colours floating high;
The noble city lent her bulwarks
  And a name that cannot die.

Venice sent her ships of prowess,
  The magic city of the sea
Could never bow to Moslem Emir,
  While a flag hung floating free.

Rome, old Rome, the pride of ages
  Lent the splendour of her name,

Pius sent his Latian vessels
   To win another page from fame.

Brave Don John, with bristling frigate
   Sailed along the firm set line,
Cheered the warriors with his counsel,
   Cheered them with the sacred sign.

And tears came sparkling, while hope's rainbow
   Covered wide the Christian host,
Tears of joy from eyes were streaming,
   Shouts from hearts that weighed the cost.

Shouts of victory from the Christians
   Along the dreadful vanguard ran,
And the prayers of millions for them
   Braced the heart of every man.

Four hours long the fight had lasted,
   Grappling steps, and murderous stride,
Crash and carnage, death unsated
   Flapped his red wings far and wide.

Then the Paynim hosts grew fainter,
   The wind rose up with angry breath,
And the foaming waves surged deeper
   With the dark behests of death.

Paled the Crescent, when the Emir
    Fell beneath the crashing deck,
And the shots ran thick and deadly
    O'er the black'ning gulfs of wreck.

And the weary waves rolled heavy
    With the hearts they bore that day;
Weary waves, so thick and ruddy—
    The ebb of that ensanguined fray.

And fair Stamboul, with pulse of horror,
    Mourns the thousands of her slain;
Othman's sons, black corses floating
    On the red and frightened main.

But Christian men from gloom and darkness
    Straight shook off their iron bands;
Twice six thousand weary captives
    Joyful seek their native lands.

And Rome, old Rome, had one more triumph,
    Like the Cæsars' march of old;
To the hill which bore Jove's temple,
    On the mighty concourse rolled.

Where erst the Labarum was planted
    On that glorious time-crowned hill,

Lie folded now pale Islam's banners,—
    The sacred standard triumphs still.

But sad Stamboul, all swathed in sorrow,
    Scarce heeds the daily call to prayer,
From her Mosques, the grey Muezzin
    Calls to those—who cannot hear.

Where sunbeams crest the azure waters,
    Nigh that glorious Grecian coast,
Fathoms deep in the Ionian,
    Lie engulphed the Moslem host.

And hearts shall ache, and bright hopes wither,
    For the white sails on the main;
And the flags, which floated proudly,
    Stamboul may never see again.

## THE ETRUSCAN WARRIOR'S TOMB.

—And loving lips then gave the fitting name
To burnished lamps, and touched with living flame
The slumbering fires, which woke so soft and bright
To gild those fictile vases with their light;
But shewed not fairer figures than stood there,
Watching the burning lamps, with earnest care;
Scarce breathing, lest the music of a sigh,
Should cause those flickering stars too soon to die.

But ah! those shadowy types must pass away,
Like the glad hearts which warm a finer clay;
But true to human love, which fain would keep
The loved and lovely from their final sleep;
The lamp, that longest bears its quivering flame,
To the loved child shall give its hope and name.

. . . . . .

For ever folded is the warp of years,
Faded the Iris tints, dried up the tears;
Affection's lamps, all quenched in dark despair,
Are with the shadows and the things that were;

The beating heart, the calm and manly brow,
The speaking lips, wear death's dark impress now.
So gently lay him in his rocky tomb,
Clad in his armour; let its gold illume
A little moment, and stern truth gainsay,
And feel as yet all has not passed away;
Lepaste, and the cantharus, bring here,
Fill to the brim for one who was so dear:
Bring alabastron, with its sweet perfume,
And painted stamnos, for his narrow tomb.
Bring amphoras of wine he loved the best,
Bring gems and offerings, to grace his rest;
A conqueror's trophies by him fitly lay,
Love, every honour to her dead must pay.

. . . . . .

Time has grown older, by two thousand years,
Since that sad hour bedimm'd by sorrow's tears,
When the Etruscan in his tomb was laid,
With fictile gems to soothe the warrior's shade;
Alone in that Necropolis of death,
In that dread silence, without pulse or breath;
In his still glory, in that depth of gloom,
Which living hearts, give only to the tomb:
And well have centuries kept that guarded clay,
Built in the living rock on that far day.

The gifted Greek a flood of genius pours,
And writes his name upon those sunny shores,
In rays of light, which not the lapse of time
Has yet erased from that most glorious clime;
But which like distant stars, shine on us yet,
And clothe our spirits with a soft regret,
That all the bright creations we have seen,
Are but the shadows of what once has been:
But all this glory not a ray could pour
On thy cold brow, or move that stony door;
Rome's legions came and past, the Goth strode by;
But all war's tramp shook not thy panoply;
Nor Io Pæan caused a pulse to beat
In the still tenant of that lone retreat.
Another age, another creed, has come;
But loving time some Ægis lent thy tomb,
And kept the shade of what thou once wast there,
The cold sad type, to shew that such things were:
Till late by chance, the home that girt thee well,
The stony door into thy narrow cell,
Once more was opened to the human eye:
But who can paint the deep intensity
Which gazed upon thee, as thy relics lay
A shade,—a breath,—but not our common clay?
The golden plate still glittered on thy breast,
With all the garniture that graced thy rest:

One moment more, that fine illusion's gone,
The form is traced on the sepulchral stone;
A thin dull coating of dark ashes shows
The Warrior's form, as in his last repose;
The breastplate lay where once the heart had been,
But little boots it now to lift the screen,
The dim dark veil, which still so dusky lies
Between this hour and those sad obsequies.



## FALLING LEAVES REFLECTED ON THE WATER.

With loving calm stole on that eventide,
  And slanting sunbeams through the tall trees fell,
Throwing their luxury of branches wide
  On the green turf; and by some wond'rous spell

The leaves all gaily glittered on the floor
  Of velvet sod, and the fast waning sun
With mellow rays through that green garniture,
  Lent them a moment's life, and then was gone.

One noble bough hung bending o'er a lake,
    Which slept in its own limpid beauty nigh;
And hush lay round, the heart dared scarcely break;
    A hush, which made life's pulse throb quietly.

That bough's green leaves are mirrored in the stream,
    Which loves to give so bright an image back;
Like some dear memory, some waking dream,
    Some gleam of gladness on life's shady track.

The wind is rising with a gentle sigh,
    And all unseen the slender fibres break;
Released from life, like emerald gems they fly
    To greet their loving partners on the lake.

Their own fair shadows to the summons rise,
    To join their kindred as they leave the air;
But ah! too soon the brief illusion flies
    To memory's shrine, and lives in radiance there.

## ILLNESS.

Birds, ye are blithely singing;
Bells, ye are merrily ringing;
Flowers, ye are busily springing;
      But not for me.

My lot is the bed of pain,
And the busy working of the brain,
And the thoughts that come, and come again;
      These are for me.

And the air hath a rich perfume,
From the flowers in their freshest bloom;
And all things say, ah come!
      But not to me.

I must tell the weary hours,
And think of the birds and flowers,
Until nature's healing powers
      Give them to me.

## IN MEMORIAM.

And thou, the bright and gifted one,
    Hast passed from earth away;
From a land of cloud and shadow
    To the light of endless day;
From the couch of pain and weariness
    Has thy sainted spirit flown,
To stand unfettered and redeemed
    Before thy Saviour's throne.

And we would not have thee back again,
    Thou who hast passed death's river,
And clothed in light dost stand beside
    The stream of life for ever;
We would not win thee back to warm
    That frame of suffering clay,
Or seek to gaze upon that smile
    Whose beam has passed away:

Or wish again on earth to meet
    That speaking soul-lit eye,
But our hearts may be in heaviness
    For friendship's broken tie:

And we may keep with steadfast hearts
    The shrine of memory bright,
Where the scroll of perished hours may live,
    Written in lines of light.


When last I heard thy failing voice,
    Those gently breathed words
Passed low and feelingly along
    Our friendship's severing chords;
Yet their memory rests upon my heart
    And the scene is graven there,
With all thy look of trusting love
    And with thine earnest prayer;


And with the sweet assurance
    Of all thou felt for me;
How doubly dear is every word,
    The last I heard from thee!
The last kind pressure of the hand,
    And the still kinder gaze,
As if it summoned to its glance
    Those pleasant by-gone days.


And seemed unto my heart to say
    I know thou'lt not forget,
But in my home, and round my hearth
    Some thoughts will linger yet,

Of her, who now must pass alone
    To that abiding bourne,
Which having riven kindred hearts
    Allows of no return.

And thou wast right, for I must change
    Before my love decays,
So shalt thou rest upon mine heart
    With the lights of other days:
On the shrine where memory's incense burns
    Thy name shall graven be,
And my thoughts will often visit it
    In mindfulness of thee.

## REMEMBER THEE.

Remember thee, remember thee!
    Oh! yes, this heart will cling
To the bright halo round thy name
    Though thou art withering;
Tho' shiver'd be the zone of hopes
    That girt thee in their thrall,
And set the galaxy of stars
    Which gemm'd thy coronal.

Remember thee, remember thee!
    Yes, thought, on zephyr wings,
Bears back the mem'ry of those dreams
    Fresh from their hidden springs;
They may not perish, though dark hues
    Have thrown their shade between,
And life may never bloom again,
    Or be what it has been.

We cannot breathe again the hours
    Whose sands have pass'd away,
Yet mem'ry still shall love to bask
    In the light of yesterday;
A shade has come and still must hang
    Over thy sunniest hours;
Henceforth thy feet must tread on paths
    That are not strew'd with flowers.

Remember thee, remember thee!
    Say, can the heart forget
The sweet sad music of its youth
    To which its chords were set?
Oh, never—still its tones return,
    Like incense on the breeze,
Or like the pure unearthly light
    The moon spreads o'er the seas.

Like voices of another world,
  Low whispering of the past,
How often have those viewless ones
  A shadow o'er thee cast;
Coming unbidden on those hours
  In which they have no part,
Save in the memories which become
  The shadows of the heart.

Enough, thou'st waken'd from the dream
  Which shed its golden light,
In sooth too briefly round thy path,
  And made all things look bright;
Apart our barks have floated on,
  Freighted with hopes and fears,
With rainbow colours on thy prow,
  Which melted into tears.

And far apart we still must sail
  O'er life's dim ocean wide,
Still driven onward by the force
  Of time's resistless tide:
Yet though my summers are but few,
  Say, will thy heart forget
The truthful and confiding love
  That hovers round thee yet?

## STAMBOUL.

"There is nothing now between me and Allah."

Day floats past on sunny azure,
    Clothed in light gay Stamboul lies,
And brightly shines the deep blue water,
    As the golden sunset dies.

Cross and Crescent have changed places,
    Mahmoud's banners float on high;
But the Christian name is graven
    Where its memory shall not die.

Swarthy Jew and haughty Moslem
    Crowd each steep and narrow street,
And the dark and time-worn pavement
    Rings the sound of Grecian feet.

Mild Hindoo and sage Armenian,
    Saxon, with his high pale brow,
Russ and Tartar, gaily mingle
    In the bright Byzantine show.

Look dreamy eyes from lattic'd casements,
    Soft sad music falls on air,
And the stately sons of Osman
    Lowly bend the knee in prayer.

Gaily fling the crystal fountains
    Feathery jets, as Iris fair;
Gaily there the shady plane tree
    Lifts its yellow leaves in air.

There the clustering vines wear amber,
    In earnest of their mellow fruit,
And fond hearts are gaily beating
    To the language of the lute.

There the many-coloured turbans
    Look afar like giant flowers,
And from the slender minarets
    Deep voices tell the passing hours.

White and green tents in the distance
    Gaily dot the summer sward,
And beside the crimson banner
    Stand the sentinels on guard.

Upon the balmy perfumed air
    The mandolin's sweet notes are borne;
And quickly shoots the light caique
    Across the wavy golden Horn.

Yet in this bright scene pale Sorrow
    With her shaded face pass'd by,
Flinging o'er its tide of gladness
    The mournful cadence of her sigh.

Her liquid eyes are looking weary,
    Fast twine the raven locks with gray,
And time and want have left stern traces
    As slow she climbs life's rugged way.

Kindly words distilled the dew drops
    From eyes almost too sad to weep;
"Gone," said she, "are all my bright ones,
    Gone—to their long and dreamless sleep."

"On the hill the stones lie thickly,
    The gloomy cypress spreads its root—
There—the eye has ceased to sparkle,
    And there—the busy tongue is mute."

Upward glanced she, and still onward
   As life's rugged path she trod;
Faintly murmuring " Effendi,
   There is nought 'twixt me and God."


## FANCY.

Alone, alone, in that inner zone
Where fancy reigns on her brilliant throne,
And fond hope brings on her zephyr wings
The radiant thoughts whose freshness flings

A crown of rays, on our passing days,
Still ever shining through life's dim haze;
And fragrant sighs of dear memories rise,
Like the golden hues when the daylight dies.

And thoughts we steep, where the waves lie deep
Over buried hours long gone to sleep;
While rainbow hues o'er the heart diffuse
The halcyon calm which life's balm renews.

There is no room for a touch of gloom,
To shade the colours of fancy's loom,
Where her spirit spreads, bright Iris threads
The air-woven tissues she deftly sheds.

And sails she free o'er a silvery sea,
Heedless if breakers around her be;
As the wild tide wafts her far and wide,
The while forgetting what storms betide.

Nor dissolve the spell she wields so well,
Its own short hour it may quickly tell;
Life's sands run fast before its blast,
And its starry rays may be soon o'ercast,
And fancy's dream for ever seem
Sunk in the eddies of time's rough stream.

## FEVER.

—And the music of other years stole past,
And a calm was breathed o'er the fever'd waste
Of the brain and heart of the suffering one,
Like the odour of flowers whose hues are gone.
Bright memories rose of a pure white strand
Fast girding the shore of a sea-beat land;
Where in silvery sheen the limpid brooks
Poured onward to ocean, through leafy nooks,
And the drear cold sandhills around it lay,
Like sentinels guarding the lonely bay.
There the green wave with its glittering crest
Proudly rolled on to the shore of its rest,
Leaving a girdle of feathery foam,
Ere it passed again to its ocean home;
As the shallow waters spread far and wide
The last faltering breath of the restless tide:
On plumed wings, the gull with arrowy flight,
Glanced gaily by, like a dream of light,
Now but dimly seen through a veil of spray,
Now winging o'er ocean his blithesome way.

How quickly has thought passed the gulf of years—
So heavily freighted with hopes and fears,
And has gently rested amid the rays
The calm glowing sunshine of childhood's days!
For memory's touch has a magic power
To paint far scenes on a feverish hour,
To light up the perished, bring back the gone
To life and to earth; oh quickly they come,
Leaving behind them the shroud and the clay,
To look as if still in the noontide of day!
But rages the fever and fast throbs the brow,
The image is passing, ah where is it now?
Like clouds in blue ether, like dew on the grass,
Or the tint on the flower, so doth it pass;
Lost in the varied emotions, which pain
And fever's quick pulses have stamp'd on the brain.

## THE DESERT PATH.

Thy path is through the desert waste,
   And thy footsteps may not stay;
Darkness is gathering round thy head,
   And thy home is far away.
Thy blood runs chill, and there is not
   Ee'n a lonely pilgrim nigh,
To watch the throbbings of thy heart
   Till its latest pulse shall fly.

The sandy sea may roll in wrath
   Its billows over thy head,
The fierce simoom its withering blight
   On thy weary frame may shed;
And angry meteors, only nurs'd
   By the desert's burning sun,
May quench the quivering lamp of life,
   Ere the wished for goal be won.

The solemn night is coming on,
   Begemm'd with many a star
The portals of that far off world
   Where nothing shall blight or mar.

Pilgrim, can'st thou, through Jesu's name,
    Look up to that bright abode?
If so, thou journey'st not alone,
    For thy way is with thy God.

But, see! on yonder drear expanse,
    There one shaded spot appears,
Blest by the pilgrim's parched lips,
    Bedew'd with grateful tears;
Go, drink the life spring, and confess
    That though thy path may be
Across the desert, there are yet
    Green and sheltered spots for thee.

Go, slake thy burning thirst and bathe
    Thy hot and fever'd brow,
And bless the hand whose mercy cared
    For such a worm as thou:
That little spot of green may fade,
    That blessed spring be dry,
But never sleeps that Holy One
    Who marks thee from on high.

In youth our hopes are Iris like,
    Connecting earth with heaven;

And craving kingdoms for ourselves,
    Which wisely are not given;
Full soon the rainbow colours fade,
    And the spirit learns to dress
And view the world in its own guise—
    In its real nothingness.

And who should mourn though earth have not
    The gloss which once it wore?
A dream it is which lulls the heart
    And quickly passeth o'er;
And then the truth which none may shun
    Reveals the dross beneath,
'Tis thus our brief span is consumed
    By hope, decay, and death.

And if we must resign the hopes
    Whose brief existence shed
A starry radiance o'er our path,
    A halo round our head;
Still life is transient, and its close,
    If not the fault our own,
Will lead us ransom'd and redeemed
    To His eternal throne,

Who bought us with His precious blood,
    And to whose eye alone
The sins, the sorrows of our hearts,
    Our hopes and fears are known;
Oh may the thorns which mar our rest
    But lead us to His side,
Who left His home on high to save,
    And to redeem us, died.

## AND THERE ARE TIMES.

——And there are times when but a single word,
From tongue unknown, will strike upon a chord
Of deepest feeling, and arouse a tone
Alas but too responsive to your own;
Awaking thoughts which might as well have slept,
And dimming eyes, which else would not have wept;
And should we conquer such dark hours as these,
Or stem the tide of nature's sympathies.
May we not turn with faltering heart to those
O'er whose loved form the thickening verdure grows;
Brood o'er the lot that they have left so lone,
And bear the sorrows which were once their own.

## TINTERN ABBEY.

The setting sun with parting lustre played
On that sweet valley deepening into shade:
And lines of dying glory faintly shed
On the old Abbey's ivy-crested head;
Through its long aisles a tide of lustre pours,
And melts in beauty on its grassy floors.
It was an hour which having felt, the heart
Owns ever after, and which forms a part
Of those sad feelings, often undefined,
Which give the tone, the colour to the mind.

The sun has set—to-morrow he will be
Up in the heaven on his bright destiny;
But stately Tintern! never more shalt thou
Shake off time's furrows from thine aged brow;
Yet shalt thou long in evening splendour dress'd,
Live in the sacred twilight of thy rest;
Long may'st thou rear thine ivy-crested head,
Proud Mausoleum to the nameless dead!

Thy pillars crumbling to the touch of time
Have only made thy beauty more sublime;
Roof'd by the starry sky, the drizzling storm
But cheers the ivy on thy furrow'd form;
More touching far than in thine hour of prime,
Ere thy arched walls were dimly veiled by time.
The wild birds, singing with melodious breath
Chant thy sad requiem—oh! 'tis life in death.

What wast thou once e'er centuries had swept
Thy beauty from thee? dull decay hath kept
Her vigil o'er thee, yet sad beauty given—
Each crested arch with time hath nobly striven.
Star of another age, well may'st thou be
Mute chronicler of man's frail destiny:
His morn of promise,—shining noon,—and then
His twilight gray, alas! returns it—when?
His night of being comes, but o'er its gloom
Faith sees a new horizon from the tomb,
And age's twilight is not sad to them
Who see through faith the Star of Bethlehem;
Follow in hope the thorny path He trod,
And look through life's dim vista to their God.

## THE SLEEPER.

Was it a dream of joy that bound the sleeper,
    And gilded an unreal world with light?
Making life's Iris tints still look the deeper,
    While paused joy's pinions in their rapid flight.

It might have been a higher, holier feeling
    That girt her thoughts with slumber's gentle chain,
To her wrapt fancy other realms revealing,
    Beyond the reach of woe or withering pain.

Say did she hold sweet converse with the dead,
    Restoring lost ones to their wonted power?
Did her sweet spirit bask in light long fled,
    Giving a charm to that most witching hour?

Or was her fancy with the loved on earth
    Sever'd by distance from her anxious view?
The stars undimm'd, that lit her from her birth,
    The beacon lights that never proved untrue.

Surely to her it was a dream of peace,
    Or never had those smiles around her flung
Such joyous halo—bidding care to cease,
    Lost in the light to which her fancy clung.

Sleep on thou fair one, I'll not break the slumber
    Which flings its sunny light upon thy brow;
Nor cause thy waking thoughts too soon to number
    The golden threads fond fancy weaves thee now.

Still people thy bright world with fairy fingers,
    It may be till the morrow's dawn, thine own;
Long as the shaded night around thee lingers,
    Reign undisturbed on fancy's brilliant throne
And bask in the bright light of thine own dreamy zone.

## MARIUS IN CARTHAGE.

—And he the haughty and the prostrate one,
Ambitious ruin—desolate and lone,
Leant silently upon a pillar's base
In misery musing o'er his darkened race,
Like a gaunt spectre o'er hope's lowly bier,
Still madly chafing at his wild career,
With gory hand across his massive brow:
Shades of his victims, look at Marius now!
Genius of Carthage, didst thou hover nigh,
And through thy wastes of ruin bear his sigh?
Oh fallen city, Afric's brilliant boast
A perished empire, and a glory lost;
The Roman eagle flaps his victor wings,
And slavery's curtain o'er thy beauty flings;
Bears from thy walls thy riches and thy force,
And leaves thee little save wrecked glory's corse.
And shall the Roman still exult to tell
How Latins fought, and how proud Carthage fell?

For Dido's city ne'er shall raise her brow,
Or chain the vanquished to her galley's prow;
On her high altars never more shall rise
The sweets of power, the clouds of sacrifice;
Carthage has perished—yet in history's page
Lives the fair record of her brighter age.
Queen of the south, thy crown is lowly laid,
Rome's lofty rival, vanquished glory's shade;
Where is the power that once such vengeance hurled?
How quenched the radiance that lit half a world!

Oh who again shall tempt resistless fate,
And on thine altars swear eternal hate?
Shade of Hamilcar! why didst thou not wait
And bar the entrance to fair Capua's gate?
Why did Hannibal, Afric's bravest son
Sheathe his dread weapon ere the prize was won?
Why did the Alpine conqueror's eagle flight
Pause on his victor course, the goal in sight;
Gods of the seven-hilled City, did your power
Shield your proud temples in that fated hour?
Did the dread Sisters in the loom of fate
Weave the dark tale of Carthage desolate?

A power forbad, or ne'er had that chief been
Content to winter in so soft a scene;

Content to pluck from his own brow the bays;
Inglorious slumber on the couch of ease;
Resign the palm which Carthage else had worn,
And tread that path from which there's no return.
Afric's bright star! thy meteor course is run,
In thickest darkness sank thy blazing sun;
And desolation undisturbed shall keep
Her watchful vigil o'er thy endless sleep.


## FAREWELL.

Farewell—if e'er again this heart should turn
To the dim past, where memory's watch fires burn;
Again the shadows of those hours shall steal,
And as I felt, teach me e'en now to feel;
Once more shall thought invest thee with the rays,
The soft bright hues that lit thine early days;
Once more shall reason mourn thy erring way.
Thou meteor star why went thy path astray?
We dare not trust a light too oft obscured:
The lonely dweller in dark walls immured

May love the star, whose glimmering could pour
A ray of light across his dungeon floor;
But he who walks in the full noon of day,
Would not delight in that pale prison ray;
So the world's pilgrim whose tired feet have knelt
At friendship's altar, and her spirit felt,
Would scorn the feelings that assume her dress,
And seek her for her own pure loveliness.

## THOUGHT.

The ocean hath its limits—not a wave
May pass the boundary the Almighty gave;
The sun hath its bright course—from year to year
Still must he journey through his given sphere;
The mountains keep their station, planets roll,
And shall till time has reached his final goal;—
But who shall check the soul from ranging space?
Where is its bound, and where its resting place?
Say who can quell that messenger of mind
The meteor thought, for swifter than the wind

Doth it not bound o'er the abyss of time,
To see the glad earth in its sunny prime?
Doth it not soar with falcon eye and bring
The lights of ages on unwearied wing?
And still it tracks the desert, stems the seas,
And flutters joyous on life's deepening breeze.

Where is thy home thou spark of Deity,
Thou wond'rous wanderer from Eternity?
Thou subtle essence which eludes the all
That ever sought to bind thee in its thrall;
Fetter the worm, still the magician flies,
Destroy the creature, spirit never dies.
What art thou—who can tame thee, by what spell
Canst thou be laid, oh thou unsearchable?
Empires have perish'd, thrones have sunk beneath
The ruthless arrows of devouring death,
Still thou hast left thy record, and hast laid
Thy potent spell upon time's deep'ning shade.

Yet thou art conquered—say is there not one
Whose still small voice thou wilt obey alone?
There is a Power can check thy wild career,
And lay thee prostrate at His feet in fear;
To own thy sad misdoings, and to crave
Pardon from Him whose power alone can save:

And He will save thee, if thou seek His face;
Will stay the recreant, elevate the base;
He will subdue, will chasten thee, and be
Thy song, thy glory through eternity.


## WRITTEN NEAR LYONS.

'Twas such a heaven of brilliant blue
   As seem'd the floor of realms above,
And thought, on faith's white pinions flew
   To Him, whose aim and end is love.

And here and there a fleecy cloud
   Was moving through the upper air,
Like a bright spirit 'scaped its shroud
   And seeking for an entrance there.

Oh for a strong plumed wing of faith
   To mount beyond the earth's blue dome;
And feel the word that men call death
   Is but the joyful summons home!

1857.

# I WOULD NOT HAVE THEE SORROW.

I would not have thee sorrow,
   As the sea of time rolls on,
If the amber waves are shaded,
   If the golden sands are gone.

I would not have thee sorrow,
   Tho' the breakers curl in foam,
And burst upon thy weary bark—
   They will faster bear thee home.

Fear not the black gulfs round thee,
   Shrink not from their angry roar;
Faith's sure pilot at the helm
   Will lovingly steer to shore.

For here no Halcyon brooding,
   Gives thy heart her dreams of rest,
Nor soothing hopes flit by thee
   In their Iris vesture drest.

I would not have thee sorrow,
  If dark clouds have come between
Thee—and the golden sunlight
  Of the days that once have been.

For light may crest the billows,
  Ere the purple shadows creep;
As eventide her silvery watch
  O'er the sleeping waves shall keep;

And living sapphires lend thee
  Rays from their midnight heaven;
While calm and solemn to thy soul
  A holier light is given.


## THE SIMPLON.

Ye beautiful clouds! how ye come, how ye go,
Now dancing in ether, now shading the snow;
Here a soft mantle, and there in waves driven,
As pure as when first it left its own heaven;
Now falling like tears from the dark eye of grief,
Till the ether comes out in still pure relief.

So the heart is relieved by nature's soft rain,
When ready to burst with the anguish of pain!
Now calls the sun home the soft fleeces that lie
Like hearts of a household along the blue sky;
While high rise the Alps, like the bands of the earth,
Proud sentinels guarding—as old as its birth;
In robes which belong not to aught else below,
Where purple and violet merge with the snow,
A soft crown of white which so fondly repays
The glance of the sun by reflecting his rays.

And we passed where the snow lay on either side,
By the green yawning gulf with its portals wide;
Fair and soft as a cushion of eider down
With its dark fringe of icicles thickly strown;
And we breathed the keen air of the glacier cold
As it lay down the mountain's steep slope unroll'd,
With its pure azure hue by the snow's white edge,
Shining on, still and cold, like a sapphire wedge.

Still our weird route lay on thro' the living rock,
On—through galleries carved in the mighty block,
With windows of ice of such glittering sheen
You might fancy the emerald there had been;
And frozen bars round the entrance lay
To guard those vaults so cold and gray.

On the plateau of snow stood the lone Hospice
In its own sterile grandeur of snow and ice,
Where the lonely Cistercian oft chants his prayer
In his vigils so calm on the midnight air;
And nought can disturb the wild solitude vast,
Save the stern dark response of the mountain blast.

But the powerful Wizard who laid his spell
Over rock and river, misty gorge and dell,
Now lies still in the pomp of his narrow bed,
The dome of the Invalides over his head;
—Just the thought that had oft soothed his hours
    of pain—
" Let my ashes be placed by the banks of Seine."

. . . . . .

And my pulse faster beat by that narrow tomb,
As all still it reposed in the chapel's gloom;
While the flags of his glory lay stilly o'er
That marble cold heart, which might never throb
    more.
Marengo! Austerlitz! hush—no sound--no wave;
Droop on, for ye shadow well your Hero's grave.

## CALCUTTA.

### 1765.

There was a groan, a shriek, a parting sigh
Breathed from those lips in mortal agony;
" Air—water—air " burst from the parting breath,
And then a pause—and then came welcome death.
On their damp brows the night of being fell;
From some half lifeless, rose the gurgling swell
Of breathing, and that deep sigh hath given
A soul release—'tis fetterless in heaven.

Yet some there were whose withering frames
    withstood
Those dungeon damps, Surajah's thirst for blood;
Death's angel smote the others—still these bear
Life's weary load; while scarce the heavy air
Can nourish being; fever's scorching fire
Had almost laid them on that fearful pyre
Of human dead,—and scarcely yet the chill
Of death was on them, but the pulse was still. .

The once bright eye was faded, sunk, and dim,
And pain was stamped upon each stiffening limb;
And beauty perish'd—in that sickening look
There was a language heart could scarcely brook;
For almost writhing seemed the slumbering clay,
So wildly horrible had been that day;
Scarcely pale death could riot in his power,
Or still the agonies of life's last hour.

And when upon the breathing few there came
The morn's pure brightness, each worn, tortured frame
So haggard, and so lifeless it did seem;
And from each eye such a wild fire did gleam,
You might have held them creatures of a dream;
Or as dread spectres of the night who rose
Uncalled, unwished, to trouble your repose.

'Twas thus they perished, but what tongue may tell
The mother's anguish for the son who fell?
Oh say what limner would engage to trace
The varied feelings in that widow'd face?
Say, who shall soothe that orphan's bursting sigh,
Or wipe the tear from a fond father's eye?
None but that power who by our sufferings here,
Weans us from things so perishing, so dear,
To give us glory in a brighter sphere!

## THE CRUSADER.

### [A FRAGMENT.]

SMALL is my leechcraft Architel,—
It cannot break that fearful spell,
Or pour a balsam on the heart
That writhes beneath such hidden smart:
Hugo de Mascie still must bear
In silent woe his load of care,
Or if thou fain a cure wouldst bring,
Trace the rank evil to its spring.
Still all is bootless; though thy power
Perchance may brighten one dark hour,
It cannot bring a true relief
To him who feeds a cureless grief.

In youth, brave Architel, we deem
That life is one unshaded dream
Of hope and joy, but sterner age
Can trace the dark hues of the page;
And can, as with a limner's art,

Portray the windings of the heart.
From good to ill sometimes we stray,
As if unconscious of the way
Our feet should tread, but must ere long
Steer for the right or choose the wrong;
Thus in their turns our passions try
Through life's whole course for mastery.

I love to see thy zealous youth
Girt with the starry zone of truth;
Ere yet thy brilliant hopes expand
Beneath time's all enchanting wand;
Yet ever in thy bosom bear
A charm that may assuage the care
Of suffering life—the master key
To sternest hearts is sympathy;
And if there be a balm for grief,
'Tis not in tears to give relief;
'Tis not in loneliness to sigh
Unheeded by a stranger's eye;
But dearer far, when some loved one
Will whisper we are not alone;
When friendship's incense sheds around
A healing balm on every wound;
For say is there such cureless pain,
That will not own its gentle chain;

That will not seek its soothing power,
Its light that breaks on grief's dark hour!
Say, is there, in this world, a heart
To bid such anodyne depart;
Who would not joy that in his ill,
There was a ray to light him still?
Oh! who would not exult to bless
The starlight of his wretchedness?

Arnulf—thou know'st De Mascie's fate,
And why he is so desolate;
Why deepens on his lofty brow
The record nought may weaken now;
Why those dark eyes no longer gleam,
Why sunk and lustreless they seem,
Save when at times they wildly show
The dark reality of woe,
And make him own that there is yet
A sorrow he cannot forget;
A shadow which must deepen still
The increasing load of woe and ill;
And still I mourn that he should sever
From all that man holds dear for ever.
And fain would I oblivion fling
Over his hapless wandering;
Fain would I give his spirit rest,
In some bright Araby the blest;

Aye, and would thither bend my path
Could I but shield his head from wrath.
My life he saved, and oft my sighs
Fall for the dreadful sacrifice
Hugo de Mascie must have laid
'Neath some unholy altar's shade;
Around him is a dark web spun,
Would that its meshes were undone!

Canst thou fathom yon dark ocean,
Or still the wild wave's ceaseless motion,
Or turn the liquid lava back
From its red molten, fiery track?
Or trace the brilliant meteor's flight
Across the deepening blue of night?
Forbid the light'nings glance to fly
Over the heaven's wide canopy?
If thou canst hope to conquer these,
Then set De Mascie's heart at ease;
But, until then, 'tis vain to strive,
The Hydra head is still alive;
And nought can crush it but a power
Higher than thine—in its dread hour.

.  .  .  .  .

She was too beautiful to stay
Wrapt in the prison of her clay,

For tho' she wore Mohammed's sign
I knew her spirit was divine;
And hardly deemed that she would bless
And light my path of wretchedness;
And she has perished, yet I'm here
A renegade to all once dear;
Yet ever in the fiercest strife
Some unseen shield protects my life;
Around my head is unpierced gloom,
My only resting place, the tomb.

I said she passed, and mildew stole
With blighting touch across my soul;
Enough—not one bright ray remained,
But the plumed spirit, chafed and chained,
And madness, with her spectre crew,
Over the prostrate Mascie flew;
And little boots it to unfold
Thoughts to such fearful demons sold.
I felt as if a fiery brand
Was firmly clasped within my hand,
And never since hath healing balm
Been poured upon that burning palm.
I suffered—suffer, since that day
When reason sank beneath their sway,

And life scarce holds a darker hour,
When mind came back, and memory's power,
And truth's clear light upon my brain
Shewed me that I had lived in vain.

For once I purposed better things,
Such as life's morning pencil brings
To deck time's vista, but stern truth
Has proved the vision of my youth
To be a phantom light as air—
A promise, which was false as fair;
The mist of early hours is past,
But memory has a halo cast
O'er blossom, which has been as bright
As aught that e'er could suffer blight;
Ere sorrow laid her leaden pall
Upon my heart, and conquered all;
Hopeless and rayless still my way,
But earth must summon home her clay;
And life, alas so wasted seem
Like the dark spectres of a dream.

Fond fools, that with the mirage play,
Life's light and gladness pass away!
Like the bright sun 'neath shading cloud,
So joy is wrapt in sorrow's shroud;

But not like him will they dispel
When he shines forth in light to quell
Dull poison vapours—hope once riven
Haply may ne'er again be given;
Or may with murky light illume
And hover o'er some cherished tomb,
Like fatuous lamp, for still we cling
Even to what is withering;
And give a fealty to the dead,
And fragrant odours round them shed;
Life's truest pulses—as death brings
A last farewell upon his wings,
Memories are merged in that dread hour
And reason whelmed by sterner power.

. . . . .

A generous deed full lightly done!
My band a Moslem fort had won;
I saved the noble Emir's life,
The last and bravest in the strife;
The deed forgot—with knightly zeal
Near Ascalon, at point of steel,
I hotly pressed a flying post,
They turned, pursued, the day was lost;
Bleeding upon the ground I lay,
Long all unconscious of the fray.—
The noble Paynim paid his debt,
And ere the fading sun had set

I woke, and felt his friendly touch
Upon my burning brow, too much
Of woe to me from that sad time
When my heart withered in its prime,
For Adah promised to become
The light and gladness of my home;
But fever, whose sirocco breath
Had led me to the gates of death,
Gave to the angel of the grave
The life I would have died to save;
Phirouz, so ordered Hussein Bey,
Was sent to guard the mountain way,
And by the hand of Ranulph fell;
The gallant youth, I knew him well—
He won his spurs when Acre fell.
You know the rest, and how I lay
Unconscious of the passing day;
Darkness and light to me the same,
While madness racked my tortured frame;
When health—such health as I could feel—
Came back, De Mascie wore his steel.

. . . . .

Now, ruin rests on Amra's towers,
And withering lie her scented bowers;
Hushed is the dreamy sound of lute,
And one melodious voice is mute;

While in my own ancestral hall,
A strange escutcheon decks the wall,
And where my brilliant fame had birth
I might have just six feet of earth:
But they who rise on others' fall
Weave for themselves a deadly thrall.
'Tis said the canker worm shall feed
On those who harm in word or deed;
On craven hearts and railing tongue,
Who love to do the absent wrong;
On natures base, who inly fear
When nobler spirits touch their sphere.
But hall and home are nothing now,
They tell me madness clouds my brow;
And be it so it will not keep
De Mascie from his dreamless sleep.

. . . . .

There is a wail upon the breeze,
I see death stalking through the trees,
And words have fallen upon mine ear
That are not fit for thine to hear.
The curtain 'twixt me and the dead
Was lifted up—my fate I read;
To-morrow's glorious sun shall rise,
The last that ever lights these eyes;
Its fading gleams they shall not see,
The pinioned wing will soon be free.

Take thou this ring; in happier days
I loved to mark its sapphire rays,
I would not hand less brave than thine
Should dim the pureness of its shine;
And well the recreant knight might quail,
At whose black touch its rays would pale;
The talisman that Adah gave
Should only guard the good and brave,
And never let this priceless sign
Be worn by other hand than thine.
My sands are speeding through the glass,
The dregs, all left, will quickly pass;
A few brief hours and Hugo's lips
Will stiffen in death's dull eclipse.

Farewell! the last time Mascie's grasp
Shall hold thee in its nervous clasp!
I hear the bugle's stirring note,
Wide o'er the tents the colours float,
Islam's black banner in its pride,
And there the Red Cross standard wide;
List! 'tis the roll of the brazen drum,
Death's harvest's ripe, rush on—they come.
Clang Atabal, and trumpet loud,
" Deus id vult," the war cry proud;
Shafts quickly sped from bended bow
Shall lay the gallant Croises low;

Courtenay, Auvergne, and Rhodolphe there,
Brave Adhemar, and Moubray here;
Proud bannerets with cross of gold,
Raymond, De Burgh, and Hubert bold;
And lances fierce must spring from rest,
And gallant hand win noble crest,
Ere turns the star of Islam pale,
Or Saladin's high heart shall quail.
The Templars fiercely swell the tide,
The Red Cross on their breasts of pride,
And Guibert with his haughty frown
Upon the Moslem rushes down;
In foremost rank, De Mascie there,
His mantle, sable, gold and vair
Full lightly on his hauberk borne;
His blazon on his surcoat worn;
And helmet with the visor high,
Like one resolved to dare and die;
With bandroll on his ashen lance,
His battle cry—" St. Hugh for France."

As calm that radiant morn arose,
As on the earth lie winter's snows,
So still and fair that brilliant host,
Too soon to fade, like winter's frost,
When melted by war's torrid frown

The loosened mass comes rushing down;
As the red tide rolls wave on wave,
While death swept off the true and brave,
'Till fear upon the Moslem fell
And fainter rose the battle yell;
So fierce the Latin force pressed on,
And Aubrey the black standard won,
And stout De Burgh his brave band led
Where thickest lay the heaps of dead;
And the foiled Saracen withdrew,
As night her loving mantle threw
Upon the dying and the dead—
Thick on that gory field outspread.
De Mascie, in the fight o'er-borne,
Lay stretched on earth, his pennon torn,
The life-blood ebbing from his side,
Untamed his iron brow of pride.
In russet gown, a Palmer gray
Askance had watched the direful fray,
And rushed to staunch the trickling stream.
Ere it had quenched life's fading beam;
And bore the noble heart away,
Whose beating pulse scarce held its clay.

.     .     .     .     .

And thou, fair empress of the night,
How calmly shines thy silver light!

In the blue ether not a cloud
Has dared thy beauty to enshroud;
And all is still beneath thy ray,
In solemn contrast to the day,
When demon passions rose in strife,
And fearful was the waste of life;
But sheathed is Malek's sabre now,
Nor passion clouds his dusky brow;
As brave as any Knight on field,
Why glares the crescent on thy shield?
Would that the Holy Cross were there,
And thine the Christian's hope and prayer!
If once the Sepulchre were ours,
We soon should crush dark Islam's powers.
St. John's stout knights are on their way
With lance and sword to join the fray;
And rumour tells of banners bright
That glittered in the morning light;
Of gorgeous tents and ensigns high,
And gay embattled squadrons nigh,
And high above Ramulas fosse
The crimson standard of the Cross:
And if the noble Kurd again
With arrows thick as summer rain;
And Saphadin—so brave and bright,
He well might be a Christian knight—

With all his Turcomans come down,
Whose tents lie 'neath Khorouba's frown,
The Teuton knights, and fierce Lorraine
Will strew their bones upon the plain.
D'Avesne, and Alberic are gone—
Proudly they lie in sculptured stone;
And time their deeds shall bear along,
Soft floating in Provençal song;
But idly fall my sighs on air,
For those who heed nor sigh nor prayer;
And I must hasten, for St. Grè,
Who bore De Mascie's form away,
Warned me the hectic flush of life
Had paled—ere closed the morning's strife.

Sadly he turned him to the tent,
And o'er the brave Crusader leant,
And heard the whispered prayer arise,
Breathed from fast waning energies;
The full moon, wrapped in fleecy cloud,
As clear and pale as spirit's shroud,
Was moving on her silvery way
In the dim precincts of the day;
His eye marked not the hallowed light
Bursting the portals of the night;
But solemnly the Palmer's prayer

Rose clear upon the midnight air,
And whispered peace to Mascie's soul,
Fast fleeting to life's latest goal;
And pointed to the Holy word
And sign which he had nigh abjured,
When he had placed upon his head
The turban, symbol dark and dread;
Though ne'er disowned his father's faith—
So triumphs the bright cross in death!
All darkness pales beneath its ray,
As midnight 'neath the flash of day;
And absolution has been given
To fit the weary soul for heaven.
And in the streets of gray Tournay,
Crosses Black, for his weal shall pray;
Pray for him who in holy strife,
Buckled in mail, had given up life;
While deep the muffled bell shall toll,
And mass be chanted for his soul.

. . . . .

The sun had risen in its force,
It lit the room where Mascie's corse
Still lay, before the earth's cold grave
Had closed upon the perished brave;
And Architel beside him leant
And gazed upon those looks unbent

In death's last struggle—still he kept
His knightly watch where Hugo slept,
Gazing upon the cold, still brow,
Where death's calm impress deepened now.
The dark eye with its meteor flash
Was hid for aye by its long lash;
The lip, scarce closed, it seemed had breath
As if in mockery of death.

   .    .    .    .    .

And they have laid him in the grave,
Wrapped in the mantle of the brave;
And the gray Palmer placed the sign,
On his low grave, of love divine;
With faltering voice and eye so dim,
Sadly chanting the parting hymn;
They laid the last of his noble line
To rest in holy Palestine.

## DOMINE QUO VADIS.

Heard ye not the wail of sorrow
   In the lowly Christian's home,
As he brooded o'er the morrow
   Midst the purple hills of Rome?

Mighty in their marble glory,
   Mighty in the lines of fame,
Mightier still in time's long story—
   Record of the Christian name.

Not a cloud obscured the heaven,
   Not a breath disturbed the air,
As the hearts with sorrow riven
   Calmly prayed the Christian's prayer.

Calmly viewed the death impending,
   Dreadful as the shape it wore;
Strong in faith the unoffending,
   Dauntless still the torture bore.

Christians to the monsters given,
    Fearless met the gory death;
And the radiant hosts of heaven
    Caught with joy the martyr's breath.

Still with some life's pulse was beating
    Warm and true to kindred ties;
But alas! how fond and fleeting
    Are the hopes which love supplies.

Loudly are the lions roaring,
    Gaunt and famished for their prey;
Round the hills stern Romans pouring
    To the lists as fierce as they.

Haste! there's safety in the dwelling
    Where the dead and living meet;
Where the hymn of praise is swelling
    To the Sandy mines retreat!

By the Appian, hosts are flying
    Onward to the azure main;
Wayworn hearts, in sadness sighing
    For homes—alas ne'er homes again.

Horror draped, death hovers round them,
    Fearful perils crowd their path;
Night Cimmerian is before them,
    And behind, dread Cæsar's wrath.

Wonder not, with purpose altered,
    Peter, from that scene of doom
Fled—as fearful nature faltered
    In that hour of Stygian gloom.

Wonder not his heart beat faster,
    Brooding o'er that scene of dread,
When in Jewry his great Master
    Meekly bowed His holy Head.

And if memory called before him,
    In bright trance, the form so dear,
Joyful as the light broke o'er him,
    He was safe—for Christ was near.

"Whither Lord? life's path grows rougher,"—
    The solemn answer met his ear,
"Upon the cross again to suffer;
    Peter—why this flight and fear."

Enough—the gentle words are burning,
  Full of life in that true breast ;
And Peter to his home returning,
  Wore the Martyr's crown of rest.


## SISTE VIATOR.

Stay, Traveller stay, young morn scarce yet distils
Her thousand glories on the Alban hills ;
Still the bright dewdrop glitters on the spray,
Type of all lovely things that pass away.
Stay, Traveller stay—I once was young as thou,
With life's gay dreams thick floating round my brow ;
Hopes round my path, all things to make me blest
And brilliant stars to light me to my rest :
Halt for a moment by this marble pile,
Reared by sad hands, the fond heart to beguile ;
This life is but the tissue of a day,
Finished in grief—a Cippus by the way.

Now echo brings no tidings to my home,
Hope reaches not the slumbers of the tomb ;
For they who twist the hemp and light the torch,

Love not to linger in death's solemn porch;
Still feed they memory's lamps with fragrant oil,
And set mute seal to life's long brilliant toil;
Ere yet they quaff the hemlock, share the deep
Unfathomed silence of our dreamless sleep.
Siste Viator ! soon the noontide blaze
Will crest those purple hills with golden rays;
Stay yet a moment, while the stately throng
To death's wild dirge in sadness moves along;
See the cleft pines shoot up in spiral light
As the loved form for ever fades in night;
And the long sad procession sinks away—
The mournful pageant of life's little day.

And now wayfarer the just rites are paid,
Fast sink the sunbeams into thickest shade;
Withered the roses, the fair garlands torn,
The sybil grief her darkest robe has worn:
Let music mourning over hopes long gone
Like the melodious death-note of the swan,
Serve as a warning voice, to make thee prize
The dreamy light which yet before thee lies;
Haste thee ! nor let the lesson of to-day
Pass like a vapour from thy onward way;
So live—that aching hearts may yet illume
With memory's torch, the darkness of thy tomb !

## VALLEY OF SEPULCHRES—PALMYRA.

[TRANSLATED.]

—And the bright sun in majesty went down,
But left behind him a most radiant band
Tinging the mountains of far Syria's land;
In the blue East the full orb'd moon arose
Near old Euphrates, and a soft light throws
O'er his flat shores, so wide and sadly fair,
For where the myriads that once sported there?
The dying splendour of that glorious day
Still lent to darkness an enlivening ray;
And the sweet freshness of that stilly night
Tempered the fervor and the scorch of light;
In the deep starry sky no breath of air
Disturbed the hush that gently brooded there:—
The shepherds had retired with their young train,
And all was moveless on the dark gray plain;
Unbroken silence o'er the desert hung,
Save when the night birds in dull cadence sung.
The darkness thickened—in the twilight's gloom,
Hovered around me phantoms of the tomb;

While the lone column and the mouldering wall
Stood solemn emblems of the fate of all.
These wrecks of ages, and the dim calm time,
In this wild scene of majesty sublime,
Stamped on my soul religion's deep impress,
And awe possessed me in the wilderness.
The mournful glory of a city fled,
The wreck of ages, and the mighty dead—
These were before me in their sadness fraught
With all the deep intensity of thought.


## THY NAME HATH PASSED.

Thy name hath long passed from the dial of time,
The shadow of death hath crept over thy prime,
Gone as a dream, or a pale cloud of even
Gemming its blue, and then melting in Heaven:
'Tis thus that our lives as brief shadows pass by,
We are pilgrims on earth, but our home is on high.
And thou—it scarce seems thy bright course can
    be o'er,

That the sound of thy footsteps shall ne'er be heard
    more;
That the musical voice and the soul speaking eye,
Are now with the thoughts and the days long gone by;
That the hopes and the feelings twined round thy
    heart,
Belong but to those—who must be as thou art.

To me, thou wast one of the sunbeams which threw
On life's early path thy soul's magical hue;
And ne'er can my spirit forget the bright hours,
When thou strewed on my pathway life's loveliest
    flowers;
O'erlooked the wide gulf that divided our years,
While watching the fountains whence sorrow brings
    tears,
Where grief's finished seal was set fast on thy brow!
Thy home midst life's shadows—and where art thou
    now!
Shrined in the ideal—a gleam on life's river,
Whose wave hath passed by—its memory never!

## "THE ROOM OF REST."

They calmly slept in their " Room of Rest,"
   While the shadows of time past on;
In their stony garments proudly drest,
   The sad types of an era gone.

A flat cap lay on each sleeping head,
   'Twas a dull dreamless sleep, and long—
A rough band bound the face of the dead,
   While a strange stony braid and strong

Fastened the robe on the quiet breast,
   Where no beating disturbed its grace;
As cold and still in their " Room of Rest,"
   Lay the dead of a mighty race.

A Knight reposed in his coat of proof,
   With a fillet passed round his brow,
And eyes turned up to the vaulted roof;
   But alas! for his prowess now.

A shield lay close to his frozen side,
  And a roweled spur girt his heel;
And he wore his iron look of pride
  As when cased in his glittering steel.

They laid him there, an unbidden guest,
  In that chamber so drear and lone;
Which he built that he might find a rest
  When his warrior day was done.

And age after age in that vaulted room,
  Those gaunt dreamless figures slept on,
Till daylight burst on the house of gloom,
  And their long charmed rest was gone.

And the spoiler came, and stole away
  The fair relics that time had left;
The sculptor's work for the frames of clay,
  Cap and glaive, all were quickly reft.

And Memory spread her folded wing,
  Quickly closed her long tablets fair,
That Shadow her dusky pall might fling
  On the wreck that still lingered there.

## BIND THE NIGHT SHADE.

Aye, bind the night shade on that brow,
For nothing else becomes it now;
Too roughly has the hand of care
Fast written his deep signet there,
For aught of beautiful or gay,
To chase the dark impress away.

The light of other years is fled,
The hopes that brightly shone are dead;
But Lethe's cup remains unquaffed,
For memory sickens at the draught;
And spite of its dark hours of ill
Dreams of the past, aye idly still;
And would not lose its all of light,
E'en to forget the darkest night.
Just as the seaman vainly clings
To his last raft, when darkness flings
Fresh horrors o'er his haggard form,
Deepening the vengeance of the storm.

And who may read dim sorrow's page,
Traced with the characters of age;
For its dark touch has still the power
To dash with age youth's fleeting hour.
Yet had I the vain wish to fling
Around thy feet each beauteous thing,
Which shines in hope's Chameleon vest,
And lulls each vagrant fear to rest;
Which oft are clothed in fair disguise,
And hide with flowers where danger lies;
Say, should I ask such gifts for thee
Though clothed in brightest witchery?
No! weary Pilgrim, tho' 'twere mine
To make such phantom pleasures thine;
They have a thorn, thou seest not,
A sting that might not be forgot;
A worm may lie beneath the gourd,
Mildew and blight be on it poured;
And though so fair and bright it seem
It still might pass—a summer dream.
Thine be the joys that do not fade,
The hope that sorrows cannot shade;
The faith to trusting spirits given
To smooth life's rugged path to Heaven.
If thou have this, fear not the blight
Which may on hope's fair blossom light.

Fear not the storm—though loud the blast
Roars for a moment—soon 'tis past;
Brace up thy heart, nor let it feel
If lurid shadows round thee steal.
At eventide, hope's mellow rays
May softly shine through sorrow's haze;
And life's dull vapours shroud no part
Of the calm sunshine of thy heart.


## EL AIDEN.

Fringed is El Aiden, with bright sunlit trees,
Shedding sweet odours on the balmy breeze,
While birds of beauty, plumed wings of air,
Warbled their matin notes and vespers there;
The wild gazelle might fleetly bound along,
Or calmly rest those spicy glades among;
And life's wayfarer there might bathe his brow
In murmuring waters, whose calm gentle flow
Onward, still onward, coursing to the sea,
A mirrored image to his soul might be
Of his own passage to eternity.

That morn the sun awoke in rosy light,
Unveiling floods of beauty, which the night,
The calm sweet night, had almost deemed her own,
Graced by the brilliant hosts that gemmed her crown,
Where ether-poised, hung high heaven's starry throne.
Bathed in his brightness, dewy morn stole on
In light and fragrance, and the flowrets shone
In their first lustre: well ye might compare
That home of beauty, 'twas so still and fair,
To man's lost Eden—ere the serpent spun
The wily web which left our race undone,
Had it not been for Him who rose to save
Man, erring man, and stingless make the grave.

Mid this sweet scene, Arabia's hardy sons
Breathed on the spicy gale their orisons;
When o'er the far horizon one dim speck,
Slowly arose to scatter gloom and wreck;
Speeds the cloud onwards,—dense and darker still,
Its lurid wings full charged with death and ill;
Dim shadow casting o'er those vales of light,
As it moved onward in its sombre flight
To wrest its deathly bulk, and steal away
Earth's fairest chaplets, fresh in morn's array.

Now bursts that boding cloud to rest upon
Herb and gay flower, till every grace is gone;
Nature's bright hues, swathed deep in loving green
Like dewdrops perished, as they had not been:
Where is that Eden now?—a wildering blight
Of desolation deepens on the sight;
For the dread Locust in his vengeful way
Hath smitten beauty with a quick decay,
And that green vale hath only shared the fate
Of others just as fair, and left as desolate.


## WEEP NOT.

Weep not for those who calmly rest,
But weep for those who live unblest;
Weep for the heart whose hopes are fled,
But weep not for the happy dead!

And weep for those who still must feel
The wasting woes time cannot heal,
In sullen wretchedness, which knows
No balm—no healing—no repose!

Aye, weep for those who still must cling
To what they know is withering;
That ignis fatuus of a mind
In very wretchedness enshrined.

And weep for those, o'er whose young bloom
Has swept the dark and fell Simoom;
Whose scorching blast has laid its blight
On all that erst was young and bright.

Weep, weep for these, if thou must weep,
Pity their sufferings still and deep,
But shed not, darkly shed, the tear
Which falls upon a hallowed bier.

Which falls for those whose hour is past,
And who have looked and loved their last,
Rather rejoice that they—forgiven
Wear now the robe of white in Heaven.

## THE GOTH IN ROME.

The gaunt wolf howls, the vulture flaps her wings
And Ruin laughs, while Horror grimly flings
Her sable pall o'er those stern walls of pride;
Shaken their rocky bulks, the rents yawn wide;
The grass grows rank amidst those marble halls,
Muffling the horse's hoof, which softly falls
Where erst the Legions in war's stern array
Marched forth to meet the Parthian; Dacia say,
Where are the Cohorts that have laid thee low?
Where are Rome's Cæsars, where her Fathers now?—
Prowls the wild beast midst the unburied dead,
The ravens croak with dusky wings outspread
O'er human bones that whiten in the sun,
Heaped round those glorious wrecks, now fallen
    undone:
Asleep the hills—e'en famine's voice is still,
And carnage red for once hath had its fill.

There stalks a skeleton, a living death,
Withered and ghastly, scorched with fever's breath;

The black skin clinging to the clanking bone;
Famine's gaunt spectre, fed on weeds alone!
Creeping in its dark wretchedness away,
With sunk eyes shrinking from the light of day.

. . . . . .

Nor Sage, nor Magian, stays thy ebbing life
With his dark rites, the fierce hot tide of strife
Bursts on thy leaguered walls, in wreck they lie,
Thy slaves look on and mock thee ere they die.
E'en darkness hides herself—the lurid light
Of burning temples scares the weary night.
Wide yawn the sepulchres of mouldering dead;
Glide the pale Manes and foul vapours shed
On all sides poison, till the murky air
Breathes pestilence; e'en murder's demons there
Have couched them down for lack of human prey!
Gapes not the gorged earth for such heaps of clay.

Death holds high carnival, the nation's queen
Weeps in her faded purple, she hath seen
Her thousand triumphs, mottled with the gore
Of half a world; the mighty ones of yore
Had knelt before her; ere the deluge burst,
While still secure she slept, the Goth had nurst
His greedy vengeance, and night draped, rushed on:
Shades of Rome's mighty! of her Heroes gone,

Could not your brazen gates have stemmed his rage?
In her long story this the darkest page!
On rolled war's gloomy wave, and fiercely swept
Murder's red scythe—Rome's mighty form had kept
Her glorious mantle round her until now;
So fades her laurel crown, and pales her haughty brow.

. . . . . .

Well hath her sleep been drugged! but yet she wakes,
The murky shadow of herself,—as breaks
Light through the tempest cloud; still hath she left,
Mixed through her age's roll of darkest weft,
A warp of glory which no time can pale:
The storms of years beat on her, and assail
Her marble ruins, where on misty throne
Calmly she reigns, still peerless and alone,
Swathed deep in shadow; her stern feud with time
But makes her what she is, in ruined might sublime!

## THE TRIBUTE OF FLOWERS.

Good Queen Blanche reineth in her haughty steed,
Fair Queen, ever true in the hour of need;
To-day all banished her sorrows and fears,
As bravely she rides into gay Poictiers!

Her steed lightly treads on daintiest flowers,
While the merry bells chime the laughing hours;
And the houses glitter with flags and gold,
As on through the streets the high concourse rolled.

On her right hand rideth her kingly son,
On her left Champagne, and then dark Narbonne,
With Crecy and Bourville of great renown;
All nobles of might speed on through the town.

And many more chiefs whose high names ye ken,
The good and the tried with their belted men;
Clad in armour bright, and in rich array
Invested Poictiers on that glorious day.

And Members of Council, stout hearts and true,
Then came slowly on, with fair homage due,
Philip de Moirol, and Clement Toutemaine,
With Preval, Saint Bruge, and grave De la Chaine.

And onward they passed through the Cloister's shade,
To list to the rites at the altar paid;
Where the mass was sung, and the prayer was said,
That blessings might rest on each noble head.

Then hied they on to the Field of Flowers,
Where the roses breathed on the golden hours;
And stern Dubuison, in his robes of might,
Stood next the fair Queen in his place of right.

And Count de La Marche had his given sphere,
Good Blanche of Castile knew the haughty peer;
And kindly she glanced upon all around,
As the gay and the brilliant thronged the ground.

Then the bells rang out, and a merry peal
Echoed loud from the old Hotel de Ville;
Alight were the windows with lustrous eyes,
Clear as the depths of their own sunny skies.

. . . . . . .

And darkness stole on, yet half draped in light,
For the crescent moon had arraigned the night;
And the Members of Council studied deep
The cause of Poictou, ere they went to sleep.

But Count de La Marche left his book of laws,
At sweet Marie's lattice to plead his cause;
Ere while he had pleaded his suit in vain,
But was spellbound still with love's subtle chain.

The roses looked on with their petals bright,
While their dewy buds drank the deep moonlight;
In that still dreamy hour he chaunted his lays,
A Troubadour's song in his lady's praise.

Then gently the casement was open flung,
Marie knew the tone, heard her praises sung;
And her sweet voice fell on La Marche's ear,
—Not the words of hope he so longed to hear—

But a mild reproof that he wasted there
Fleeting hours, to justice and truth so dear;
When the grave and good were studying nigh,
The cause of Poictou, they had met to try.

And the young noble felt her words were truth,
And knew that delay might bring grievous ruth;

So he went to study, till morning's rays
Wrote their golden story on night's dim haze.

．　　．　　．　　．　　．　　．

Now Parliament sat in the Rose parterre,
The learned and wise a just cause to hear;
Guienne and Poictou were but ill agreed,
And the good Queen came to assist in need.

The will of the Vidame was closely tried,
Lest justice or right should be set aside;
And La Marche has nobly pleaded the cause
With the right and might of the kingdom's laws.

And he won for Poictou; for persuasion hung,
Inspired by love on his eloquent tongue;
And the Regent questioned who led him on
To plead the good cause, so right nobly done.

He said it was Marie whose mild reproof
Had set him to ravel the tangled woof;
And the Queen strait promised that gentle hand
Should be his, with title and dower of land.

And in memory bright of that sunny day,
Good Blanche laid a tribute, full sweet to pay;
A tribute of roses, fair queenly flowers,
To recall the hues of those earnest hours.

And each stately member low bowed his head,
While her loving voice its gay missive spread,
And for long years did " La Baillée des Roses,"
To the Members of Council its sweets disclose.

And Time's mighty river rolled fast away,
Yet still gaily did France her homage pay;
Until strife arose between prince and peer,
As to precedence in a cause so dear.

Then the graceful observance past away
Like the morning dew on the roses' spray;
For the League forbad by a stern decree
That the beautiful Rite e'er again might be.

## THE LAST SLEEP.

She sleeps her last long dreamless sleep;
And ye—have ye yet tears to weep?

She was our own but yesterday,
So loved—oh! can that form be clay?
Death's heavy impress hath been set,
But still some glory lingers yet.

Long anguished nights I had not slept,
But ceaseless vigil by her kept;
I knew that she must pass away,
I felt the idol was but clay,
Yet still I worshipped, for we cling
Closer to what is withering;
I marked the fevered pulse's strife
Waging its hectic war with life;
And painting on her cheek the bloom,
Alas! sure herald of the tomb;

I knew the lustre of that eye
Would soon be lost in vacancy!
And that her pale and queenly brow
Would look, alas! as it looks now.

Unwearied still I marked the close;
I wished not, wanted not repose;
To waste the fleeting precious time
Which still was hers, had been a crime.
Oh who would scorn the feelings given
To bear us up, ere yet be riven
The plank—which bears us on the wave,
The hope—between us and the grave.

. . . . . .

Stilled is the tumult of that breast
Thus early gathered to its rest;
Life's sunny dreams once bound that brow,
The pure white grave cloth binds it now;
How cold it strikes upon the heart
To look upon thee as thou art!
And yet I cannot cease to gaze
While still the dying sunset rays
Fall faintly on that sculptured face,
And lend those lines a sorrowing grace;
Just as ye see in some old pile,
The soft light stream along the aisle.

Falling on marble weepers there,
In all the guise of deep despair.
A shade rests sadly on those lips,
Sunk are those eyes 'neath death's eclipse.
That voice, with more than music's tone,
Love's sweetest echo—now is gone.

. . . . . .

Years are fast crowding on that face,
Full soon its lines ye may not trace;
Oh let me once, but once again
Lay this o'er-weary burning brain
On that so cold and marble brow!
Would it could cure my fever now;
Which soon must make me what she is.
Avaunt—who dares deny me this?
Ah me! this heart can scarcely brook
The moveless form, the altered look;
Another glance—oh let me place
That ruffled fold in quiet grace;
I've strewed bright flowers along thy way,
And I must smoothly wrap thy clay.
It creeps along my nerves to think
These eyes could gaze on thee, and shrink;
To feel that thou art past my care,
When once I lay thee stiffly there;
And know my life's one dreamy spell,
Is folded in that last farewell.

## FEAR NOT.

Fear not, tho' Time's shadows fast lengthen,
   Though Life's sunbeams but scantly fall;
Though the bright flowers have closed their petals,
   And night hastens to weave her pall.

Though the birds, whose throats are all music,
   Float not softly by on the breeze;
And fast the sear tints of the autumn
   Are flung o'er the face of the trees.

Though no zephyrs breathe softly round thee,
   And skies wear a dull ashen hue;
Fear not the dull folds of the vapour,
   The shadow will pass from the blue!

And reveal the bright home beyond it
   Where the stars for ever shine on,
To pour their calm rays upon thee,
   When the day's changing hues are gone.

Fear not the fast deepening twilight,
  Let it breathe on thy soul its calm;
And the dark fretting thoughts which sleep not,
  Shall be dipt in a healing balm.

And though darkness fold round thee deeper,
  The far Heaven will but brighter be;
And morn's dewy hour feel the sweeter,
  When its glory breaks forth on thee.

## BOABDIL'S FAREWELL.

. . . . . .

FLUTTERED gaily silken standards,
  Gaily floated costly plumes,
As on fierce and sable charger
  Leon his stern watch resumes.

White tents glitter on the Vega,
  Floats each banner's broidered fold;
And afar the dark Sierras
  Shine with dying sunset gold.

Blazed the Five lights on the turrets
    Ere the crescent moon arose;
Gilding pale the lofty summits
    Where Nevada piles her snows.

Moorish towers cast gloomy shadow
    On the plain that sleeps in light,
Where the steel clad squadrons glisten
    And high wave their pennons bright.

There—dark eyes flash forth defiance,
    This no gentle tilt of reeds;
Sets in gloom our star for ever,
    And the fierce El Zayra bleeds.

Whistling fly the venomed arrows,
    Fast the bravest lances fall,
Starts the horse without his rider,
    As the Lombards strike the wall.

Calmly o'er those warring squadrons,
    Faint the waning even smiles;
As poured Hamet's dusky Zegris
    Through Algaro's dark defiles.

War clouds deepen on Granada,
   Shines the Vega thick with steel,
And the watch fires dimly burning
   Jaded Moors' dusk brows reveal.

Fiercely charged the stern Gomeres,
   Clanged their death note trumpet-loud;
But before the haughty Spaniard
   Melt they fast like summer cloud.

  .    .    .    .    .    .

There is a sound of bitter wail
   In stern Granada's towers;
And hushed the song and castanet
   In her gay myrtle bowers.

Silver lamps shed dreamy twilight
   Gleaming on those scented flowers;
And afar the winding Zenil
   Murmurs to the moonlit hours.

Once, but once again—Boabdil
   Looks around his marble hall,
Where the pale citron droops its leaves,
   And the Iris fountains fall.

His flashing eyes are dark with grief,
  As they light his burning brow;
The Christian hosts are on the plain,
  And he dares not linger now.

For Avila's stately Bishop
  In his pomp hath passed along;
And halts before the fretted gate
  With a brave and stately throng.

Then bursts the moan of bitter grief
  As the Spaniard marches in;
"Take, take possession of our land,
  For we lose it by our sin."

And soon upon our Moorish towers
  Ye will plant your silver cross,
And our gold, it is so heavy,
  Well your king may count it dross.

Yes, ring loud your shouts of triumph,
  As your flags wave in the van;
And sing on the songs which tell me
  I must live a banished man.

I march on to meet your great ones,
  The fallen king must homage pay;
And my glorious Alhambra
  Be a home for Christian clay.

Bright and beautiful Granada!
  Inch by inch we fought for thee;
But 'twas willed the Cross should triumph,
  And the Moslem bend the knee.

Lost for ever! fair Granada,
  Pride and glory of this Spain;
Moorish hearts bled bravely for thee,
  Bravely fought, but fought in vain.

. . . . . .

So he passed from out the portal,
  And fast gained the Signal hill;
But on the flowery Vega,
  His dim eyes lingered still.

The bright sun lent his farewell rays
  Just to gild a moment yet,
Those lofty towers and minarets
  Ere in evening robes he set.

And o'er that cope of brilliant blue
  A vapoury shadow fell;
As the voice of the signal gun
  Tolled the Moorish kingdom's knell.

And hot and fast the bitter tears
  Answered to that fearful sign;
"Alla Achbar!" sighed Boabdil,
  "When did sorrows equal mine?"

## THE DEPARTURE.

Away, away! the morning light is breaking
  In waves of gold on thy ancestral trees;
The glossy ivy on the towers is waking
  To the sweet whispers of the balmy breeze.

Away, away! the hues upon the mountain
  Lie folded thick upon its jagged side;
Away—while yet the plumed jets of the fountain
  Are thickly dashed with Iris tints of pride.

Away! the wild birds are in chorus singing,
   Midst the green homes which they have charmed
      so long;
From the far tower the bell for Lauds is ringing,
   And through dim aisles soft floats the matin song.

Loud caw the rooks, long have their dark wings
      floated,
   The ebon tenants of those trees of yore;
The stately herons, near the mansion moated,
   Stalk proudly on its sweeps of velvet floor.

On the wide lake the white swan, from her rushes,
   Moves o'er its calm like some fair dream of light;
And from green quivering boughs, the busy thrushes
   Pour on the slumbering air their young delight.

Upon the slopes the cedars cast deep shadow,
   Girt with a glory gathered from old time;
The purple crocus gems the upland meadow,
   Laden with dew drops born of morning prime.

The owls fly past, from daylight to the tower,
   Swathed thick in ivy, growth of elder years,
Alike disdainful both of sun and shower,
   They moping fly, as if weighed down with fears.

                                      K

The mastiff howls at thy untimely going,
    With loving instinct to thy lordly race;
The hooded hawks, with idle jesses flowing,
    Perch drooping by, as gone their pride of place.

In the rich oriel the wind harp is playing
    In mournful cadence to thy parting feet;
And in the panell'd hall, mute lips are praying,
    Pale mourning statues near the oaken seat.

The Dais is empty—graceful figures gliding,
    No more shed smiles on those who laugh below;
No clash of arms, as fresh from tilt or riding,
    The stately nobles liberal largesse throw.

All round thee hang the shades of the departed,
    Rich in their costly robes and courtly grace;
The painter's skill hath left thee the high hearted,
    Dim centuries' gathering of thy noble race.

Let their looks teach thee deeds of knightly daring,
    As soul greets soul through those clear life-like eyes;
And that fair pallid face, its heart grief wearing,
    Lift thy sad thoughts to realms beyond the skies.

Dost thou not feel the pressure of those fingers,
   As on thy glossy curls that hand was laid;
Doth not thy pulse beat faster as it lingers
   To catch the whispered prayer so often said.

That form, so graceful in its airy lightness,
   Now resteth clay cold in its marble shrine;
That look, which centred on thee in its brightness,
   Can joy no more in the sweet grace of thine.

Look, till thine eyes are shaded by the grieving
   For thy lost treasures and stern path so lone;
Then pass—the first sad step to thy achieving;
   First win thy spurs, nor faint till all is won.

Well may'st thou gaze—those softly drooping lashes
   Thou ne'er hast dewed with sorrow's glittering tears;
No whispering voice reproves from kindred ashes,
   Nor justice meets thee swathed in sombre fears.

'Tis well to be at peace with the departed!
   Lest some sharp thorn we planted in the breast,
Might by some chance, have passed away, and started
   Up in our own, to mar our spirit's rest.

Thy soul is swathed in shadows, but hope weaveth
    A veil of rosy light, sometime to be
Flung o'er the heart that now so sorely grieveth;
    As life's dark wave too roughly beareth thee.

That chiselled face still nobler in its sorrow,
    Rich in the impress of thy lineage high,
Bears on its front the promise, that a morrow
    Shall see thy drooping banner proudly fly.

Heed not the frowns of those who still would bless thee,
    The while thy pennon floated on the keep;
When fortune smiles full fain they will caress thee,
    Joy in thy joys, and for thy sorrows weep.

Brace up thy heart, adversity hath arrows
    In her black quiver, which thou hast not known;
The straiten'd hand, the shivering thought that harrows
    The noble heart when its high hopes are gone.

Thy grey haired servitors are passing over
    To other masters than those loved so long;
In time thine eyes will waken to discover
    The sunken rocks that wrought thy house such wrong.

The brave escutcheon for a little longer
　　Hangs on the wall, with all its quarterings fair;
And then the stranger—stern change makes him stronger—
　　Comes in with pomp, to make his new home there.

. . . . . .

Go to the chapel where thy dead are sleeping,
　　Shrined in the marble which secures their fame,
In their cold dust a noble record keeping,
　　To rouse in hearts like thine a kindred flame.

There pay thine Orisons, while yet the dial
　　Warns with dark shadow thy young feet away;
While o'er thy heart rolls the deep flood of trial,
　　Let these mute figures nerve thee for life's fray.

From storied windows the stained glass is throwing
　　Its rich warm hues on sculptured faces there;
Gilding the calm of ages with its glowing,
　　And thy young face—almost as marble fair.

Now let the pulses which beat high still make thee
　　More and more worthy of the name thou bears;
Shorn of thine acres, let the thought awake thee!
　　To deeds and daring which may mate with theirs.

Look not again on the broad fields around thee,
    On the proud castle cresting the green steep;
Burst is the chain which erst had bravely bound thee,
    But still undimm'd thy blazon on its keep.

Let not the arrow in thy soul sink deeper
    Than needful goad, in search of honor, fame;
And though life's onward path may be the steeper,
    It will but add a halo to thy name.

Grant the weird Sybil's words so fitly spoken
    Be still the chart thy daring feet would tread;
Still keep thy noble heart's high faith unbroken,
    And then come back to gaze upon thy dead.

Come with the gold, whose glitter may restore thee
    The halls and lands in other keeping now;
Come to the hearts who bitterly deplore thee,
    With fame's bright chaplet woven round thy brow!

## SICKNESS.

The still night lay folded round me
   In that dark and silent room;
And fast upon my spirit fell
   Dim shadowy waves of gloom.

The past with myriad echoes
   Came floating dreamily by;
And the wind through the slumb'ring beeches
   Stole calm as a spirit's sigh.

The fevered heart's quickened beating
   Fell fast on the listening ear,
And stillness crept closer round me,
   Till it wore the robe of fear.

But over the midnight heaven
   Passed a flood of silvery light;
As the stars in their glory shining
   Sent a music along the night.

As balm on my troubled spirit,
  The light of that starry zone
Stole over earth's weary fret work,
  Like rays from before the Throne.

And I laid me down in quiet,
  All unheeding the cares that lay
With their folds of cloud and vapour,
  O'er the life of the coming day.

And oft since that tide of sickness
  In its sadness and depth of power,
Hath mem'ry winnowed a lustre
  From the light of that solemn hour.

## IDA.

Loud roared the wind, and fearful night
Had dimly veiled dark Ardoch's height;
As sternly from its craggy steep
Its time worn towers o'erlooked the deep;
A storm was gathering deep and loud,
Loomed black as night the thunder cloud.
And fast the gloomy darkness fell,
As louder boomed the ocean swell;
And nearing fast that iron coast,
Like feather by the tempest tost,
A stout ship made unwilling way
To Gordon's steep and craggy bay.
Fierce o'er the dull and leaden sky
The fiery writing gleamed on high;
And the loud thunder's awful roll
Sounded like knell of parting soul.

The signal gun's faint dying peal
Upon the harrowed senses steal,

And wreaths of foam upon the rock,
As stern it met the tempest's shock,
Looked like grim smile on marble face,
Which leaves not one faint loving trace;
Mocking the weary soul to feel
The heart beneath as cold as steel.

Oh 'twas an awful sight to see
That fair ship in her agony;
As crashing fell her mighty mast
Like reed before the tempest blast;
While yawning gulf and roaring wave,
Fast shrived the hearts so true and brave;
The sweeping blast their requiem said,
And surging wave quick shrined its dead;
Their winding sheet the white sea foam,
Meet vesture for that ocean home;
And sea birds grim loud shrieked their wail,
Faint echoes of that furious gale.

With eager step a little band
Of quivering hearts had sought the strand,
With torch and rope and seaman's gear,
Fast gathered in that hour of fear;
But all too late—the moaning wave
Sang its wild dirge above the brave.

The shivered spars and floating mast,
Like ciphers o'er the wild sea cast,
Were all that then remained to tell
The death fight with the billows' swell.

Not all—for pillowed on the foam,
A little craft had found a home;
Cradled hope of a dying heart—
Well from stern eyes the tear might start,
Life's pulse should in that frail bark be,
A waif upon that surging sea!
The sea weeds gathered closely round,
As if to guard the sleep profound
Of that sweet babe, a faint relief,
Dim smile, on that huge soul of grief!
And calm she lay, that ocean gem,
So roughly rent from parent stem;
Dark sorrow's gift! ah, who may know
What thy stern heritage of woe?
But long as Gordon's castled steep
Frowns on the dark and solemn deep,
His hall shall yield thee shelter, rest,
Till dearer homes shall claim their guest.

Full softly nurtured had she been,
As eager eyes could tell, I ween;

And cambrics fine and costly lace
Showed that she came of gentle race.
Moons came and went, and fair she grew,
And loving spells around her threw;
And fondly did her young heart pay,
The love showered on her since the day
Of awful wrath, and raging power,
When first she slept in Gordon's tower.
And yet, so feeling loved and blest,
Within her stole a deep unrest;
A sad soul,—longing yet to know
What passed before that strife of woe;
Who once had loved her, whence she came,
Her lineage, and fond parent's name?
Oh who was she?—the good and fair,
Who nurtured her with jealous care,
Could only tell her the dark tale
Of struggling ship and whelming gale.

Moons came and went, and sun and shower
Had ruled in turn the passing hour;
And morning rose, and evening fell,
Came greeting bright, and sad farewell;
And all that makes the sum of years,
Their robes of joy oft bound with tears;
Bright hues of life so gaily worn,

Dim faded hopes which can't return;
Young life's momentous busy dream
On Ardoch's height passed smooth I deem.

And fair those loving sisters grew,
As gentle time fresh graces threw;
Sisters in love, though not in race;
The soft pink hue upon the face,
Quick mantling like the rosy light,
Spoke Scotland's child, so clear and bright;
One well might deem those azure eyes
The reflex of her own blue skies;
Those golden locks you might have thought
From the deep glowing sunbeams caught;
And the bright tint upon each cheek,
So painted by the crimson streak,
Shorn from the sun, as he sank down
To wear his glorious western crown.

Ida—the name her friends had given
The gem, from ocean's dark wave riven—
Unlike her sister sylphs so fair,
Looked like some sweet exotic rare;
As if she longed for warmer skies,
Which lent their glory to her eyes;
So deep, so bright, they seemed to crave

A home beyond the salt sea wave;
While on her paler cheek there fell
Dark waving curls with subtle spell;
The carmine tint would come and go,
Giving her cheek a deeper glow;
So subtle, delicate and fair,
As roses lay in ambush there.

And when her laughing sisters flew
To cull bright flowers where'er they grew;
And rifle as with fairy spell
Old ocean of sea-weed and shell;
She followed them with wistful eyes
Delighting in their glad surprise;
And resting on some rocky steep,
Whose hoary crags o'erlooked the deep;
With looks intent upon the wave
As though her glance might reach some cave,
Deep, deep, beneath the rolling sea,
Where human hearts might shrined be.
The heart whose pulse had been her life
Ere quenched in that dark ocean strife;
For neath those waves of lucid green,
Swathed in long bands of glittering sheen,
Pillowed by rock and pearly shell,
Lay dreamless those who loved her well.

And oft her sweet and solemn prayer
Was said to soothe the sleepers there;
Till fancy's brooding eye could see
The shapes that ne'er again might be;
Thus over her young being stole
A softened light, a dream of soul,
In which she moved,—tho' loving all,
Still on her life there fell a thrall;
A deep, deep longing in her heart
For those of whom that life was part;
The loved and lost—thus like a dream
Her own fair life did often seem.

.   .   .   .   .

Grey Ardoch's castle, strong and fair
Still lifted high its towers in air;
Crowning the stern and massive sweep
Which set its front against the deep;
Laving those sullen crags and caves,
Worn by the never resting waves,
That toss their feath'ry jets of foam
'Gainst Gordon's proud and rocky home;
But sometimes like a silvery lake
Would in clear loving ripples break;
When e'en a fairy skiff might glide
O'er its heaven of waters wide,

And only dreamy zephyrs wake
The calmness of that salt sea lake.

There Ida lives, a graceful flower,
Sweet blossom culled in stormy hour;
With Gordon's blooming daughters fair,
Life of his life, from year to year;
No quivering lips had come to claim
And to her give a dearer name;
And little mention passed I ween
Of a dark hour which once had been;
Though ever in that sea-bird's breast
Was nourished still a hopeless quest;
Till once again on Ardoch's steep,
Grim ocean's voice rolled loud and deep;
Tossed to and fro his angry main,
Till the hushed breakers woke again;
And with one huge and mighty reach
Stranded a vessel on the beach;
If beach those craggy rocks could be,
The land line 'twixt the earth and sea.

. . . .

The tissue of our lives is change!
How often in life's daily range
Dim shadows cloud its sunny bloom!

Yet still athwart its hours of gloom
Stars glimmer in our leaden sky
And silv'ry moonbeams gleam on high;
Not always erring mortals know
What truly makes their weal or woe.

Morn rose, and ocean looked as fair
As if no storm had brooded there;
And inmate now in Gordon's hall,
A guest, of foreign port and tall,
Sat welcome at his festive board,
With chosen viands amply stored;
Fresh also there in morn's array
His children, beautiful as day;
And Ida, brighter if less fair,
Might with those loved ones well compare;
—Sudden on Rudolf's heart there fell
At once some deep and subtle spell;
Within him woke a strange unrest
A fluttering in his troubled breast;
Ever o'er his spirit stealing,
Thoughts, still deeper thoughts revealing;
As sought he in that loving eye,
Faint reflex of sad hours gone by;
And in that cheek of deeper hue,
As if from warmer skies it drew

Its sunny glow—ah, what her name?—
To quivering lips the question came.

Few moments soon sufficed to tell
The tale of years, and what befell
In weary vigil on that night,
When Gordon sought his Castle's height;
Wrapt in his swaging arms a life,
Sole relic of that fearful strife;
And how in vain he sought a trace
Of friends, of kindred, or of race;
Who still might claim a fairer power,
To love and shield his ocean flower:
But all in vain his earnest quest,
And still a loved and loving guest,
That foreign plant, so sweet and fair,
Was blooming bright in Scottish air;—
So light and gladness sometimes burst,
From storms by thickest darkness nurst.

Have ye ne'er seen a cheek turn pale,
As on the ear fell spectre tale;
Some deed of darkness or dismay,
A struggling in these hearts of clay
To trace some deep forbidden lore;
Dim pastime in the days of yore?
—So lingered not a tender streak,

So blanched the life tint on the cheek;
And scarcely breathed that little band
As round that stranger guest they stand.

Not always aching hearts have power
To tune them to the passing hour;
Not always can faint quivering words
Find voice upon life's straining chords;
The fluttering thoughts oft beat in vain,
Against their prison house of pain;
Till freed at last, in happy hour
Bright words descend in healing shower;
So Rudolf thus life's tangled braid
Unravelled from its years of shade.

" In that gorgeous land, where the sea bird flings
Soft flashes of light from his golden wings;
And the shining pearls in their beauty sleep,
In their silent homes 'neath the amber deep;
Where the beauteous creatures the waters hold,
Are shaded with emerald, tipt with gold;
And all hues that in earth or air there be
Seem to gladden thy wastes, thou deep, deep sea!
Where the wondrous stars in clear glory lie,
The bright far worlds of the midnight sky;
And the lustrous gems lie shrouded from sight,

In primal homes in the caves of night;
Where the scented breeze bows the waving palm,
And the heart is steeped in an odorous balm;
Where the gauzy butterfly floateth by,
Like a summer thought, or a fragrant sigh;
Midst feathery plants in their graceful swell,
Blushing bright to the breeze ere it softly fell;
There, Ida—clad in the gay hues of earth,
Far o'er the sea, lies the land of thy birth."

" But fell a thick cloud o'er that sunlit scene,
For sorrow's dark quiver holds arrows keen;
And pale sickness came with a withering blight,
And the young and fair passed away from sight;
Till the hearts thy parents had called their own,
Slept side by side 'neath the sculptured stone;
So sought they the last lovely gem to save
By bearing her over the Indian wave."

" Moons passed away, and the sun in his sweep,
Kissed o'er and o'er the red waves of the deep;
But tidings came never, and drooping hope died;
Alas for the heart so shorn of its pride!
And sickness of thought, and sadness of soul
Deeper and stronger o'er Reginald stole;
His morning dream had come to its waking

Gloom thickly wrapped the heart so fast breaking,
And daily he died, for nought could restore
The life of his life, 'twas sapped at the core;
And the dreamy light in his starry eyes,
Fast faded away as the sunset dies;
For grief deeply swathed in her raven plume,
Marked his forehead fair with the seal of doom;
And like vision pale he more lovely grew,
As nearer the spirit's pure land he drew.
I well knew his bright wings were plumed for flight,
And he passed—as morn touched the verge of night;
His sorrows forgot, we saw not a trace
Of life's long woe on his beautiful face;
And all that for me on this earth could die,
Like dream of night, passed away with his sigh.
—In silence they carved out his narrow cell,
By the sweet young flowers he loved so well;
The plumes of the palm gently waving o'er
The dear form we should see on earth no more;
And bitter and fast fell a brother's tears,
For the good and brave, the loved of long years;
Nor left he that land, till a marble shrine
Lay firm and fast on that mound of thine.—
To this way worn heart, the wide gulf of years
Hath borne this sweet flower, on its tide of tears;
When her loving tones on the stillness broke,

My slumbering thoughts in their might awoke;
And all quickly pass'd through my wildered brain
A thrill which knit faster life's early chain;
And its kindred links have but brighter grown
As each rushing moment hath quicker flown;
Had the loved and the dead been here to claim
This beautiful flower to bear their name;
I need not more proof, if such proof there be,
Love claims the bright gift of the surging sea."

We pause not in our simple tale
To say what rose-leaf cheeks turned pale;
Nor in the depths of starry eyes
How mingled sadness and surprise;
What questions asked, what thoughts exchanged,
How busy fancy idly ranged;
That Gordon's grave and tender look,
The thought of change could scarcely brook;
And Ida and her sisters deemed
The tale so strange, they surely dreamed.

And soothly did good Rudolf tell
The varied lines that him befell;
Of Reginald, and how they fared,
By time but more and more endeared;
Young orphans left, had sprung to fame,

Moubray, their parents' honoured name;—
The woe, when came the hour to part,
The wrench, that tore that noblest heart,
When to save Ida's precious life,
Her own fast fading in the strife,
The mother bore her child away,
As eventide was wrapt in gray:
How night upon their spirits fell,
Not Rudolf on that scene could dwell—
Yet for a time—oh say not years!
Hope sometimes mingled with their fears;
But love upon untiring wing,
No trace of that brave ship could bring,
Which erst had spread her dreamy sail
To win the breath of the spicy gale;
Still useless all, no tidings came,
But anguish stern, and hope in vain.—
At last that heart of hearts gave way;
The dark cloud deepened day by day,
And it needs be, by sorrow nurst,
The breaking heart must sometimes burst.

. . . . .

Oh life! thou many sided dream,
Shadow and sunshine, storm and gleam;
An Iris, nurst by darkling shower,
Or zephyr calm to rule the hour;

Still must thy sands speed through the glass,
Still warnings o'er thy dial pass;
Onward still, and still for ever,
Down the immemorial river;
On—the silent steersman steering;
Onward,—to the unseen veering;
Still bearing to the shoreless main
The hours well spent, or spent in vain;
Nought is still but the tideless sea,
Which girdles round Eternity.

. . . . .

Speak we of change, for change hath come
O'er Gordon's happy Highland home;
For now a bark is on the main,
And broken youth's sweet subtle chain;
Nor may we dwell upon the tears,
In memory of fair childhood's years,
Suffusing those bright orbs of light,
As Ardoch passed from Ida's sight.
No more she heard the billows swell,
Or Gordon's last deep toned farewell;
Though still his voice upon her ear,
Fell like faint echo, calm and clear.
And still upon her heart his look,
Which met again, she could not brook;

And little solace was it then,
To say her eyes might once again
Rest fondly on that cherished home ;—
For quickly cleaving the white foam,
A gallant boat with sunlit sail,
Wide spread to catch the western gale,
Was bearing her young heart away
From Scotland's crags, and mountains gray.

But love stood closely guarding by,
And Rudolf gently swaged her sigh ;
Nor sought he idly then to quell,
Dark sorrow for those loved so well ;
But whispered words of hope and cheer,
In soft low tones to meet her ear ;
Well might she trust that noble face,
So rich in every thought and grace ;
Though time had left his missive there ;
And midst the waves of raven hair,
Pale silvery lines were woven fast,
Sorrow's keen record of the past.
Her sister too, with eyes of light
Sat by her weaving visions bright,
Fair pictures from quick fancy's loom,
To chase away her spirit's gloom ;
The airy web the young heart weaves

Ere life's fresh thoughts are bound in sheaves;
Ere sorrow's cold dull shadow threw
A cloud to mar their heaven of blue;
Or time's stern wisdom taught to dress
This passing scene in nothingness.

 .  .  .  .  .  .

Again we fold the warp of years,
Spangled with joys, or dewed with tears;
Fast turning down another leaf
With all its lines of joy and grief;
Thick dashed with sprectral thoughts which tell
The tale of years remembered well;
With clearest rays of starry light
Or sorrows drest in shades of night.
'Tis thus the thread of life wears on,
Until its faded hues are gone;
Days quickly wake to set in sleep,
Fast flowing onward to life's deep,
Till all its varied pictures pass,
Like vapour on the polished glass;
The race, in shine or shadow run,
Must reach the goal—its future won.
Still Ardoch with its time-worn towers,
Over the restless ocean lowers;
And still the sun at eventide,

Impaints the waves with golden pride,
And sheds its thousand opal dyes
As in glorious shroud he lies;
—The moon still lends her silver band
Like spirit path, to brighter land;
And o'er that waste of waters blue,
Every wave is fringed anew
With the flickering shades of even,
As day is lost in night's deep heaven.

The mountains on the southern side
Still lift on high their crests of pride;
And o'er the changing hues of day
Pale clouds their airy revels play;
While nearer yet the hill's dark line
Is thickly girt by belts of pine;
And larches tall like giants stand
With waving plumes, a mighty band:
The yellow broom laughs glittering nigh,
And purple heather breathes its sigh;
And harebells with their wealth of blue,
Around a sapphire lustre threw;
All drest in hues of light, young flowers
Breathed odours on the passing hours.—
Waved blithely flags on that sea pile,
And Ardoch wore its fairest smile,

When Gordon gaily welcomed o'er,
His Edith from stern Nordland's shore;
Grey Nordland—where the red fire's gleam
Pales all the stars with ruby beam;
And where the shining glaciers keep
Their ages' watch on mountain steep,
Cresting the dreamy wastes of snow
With sapphires of the noontide glow :
Where hearts of price, the brave and free,
The North men of the wintry sea,
Still lash their white sails to the mast,
And dauntless brave the icy blast;
The sea kings of that rocky coast,
Old Norway's stern delight and boast.
His Edith still,—tho' changed her name
For one—a part of Scotland's fame;
Had come once more, a dream of light
To bless the loving gazer's sight;
Eftsoons, to wear upon her brow,
Withal so fair and queenly now,
A coronet, still more to grace
The Gordon's brave, time-honoured race.—
For aye—we leave that rock built home,
Cresting those watery sweeps of foam;
So rich in noble hearts and true,—
Time wanes—the spells, that round us threw

Their airy threads, are breaking fast,
My tale, alas! is with the past;
Yet still, a word—some memory given
To the fair pearl from ocean riven!
Softly the waves of raven hair
Still float adown her forehead fair;
And still the same deep magic lies,
In the calm glory of her eyes.
The dreamy light whose potent spell
Was cast in years remembered well,
When Gordon's cordial home and hearth
Bounded her all of light on earth;
O'er her sweet life the deeper tone,
Wrung from those days, was still her own;
Like some bright Cynosure whose ray
Won all true hearts within its sway,
And gilding Rudolf's passing days,
Like sunlight through the folds of haze:—
Let fancy from her golden loom
Weave tissue of the brightest bloom;
And genius its enchantment shed,
And taste her Iris meshes spread.
As Ida moves, a dream of light,
The evening star to Rudolf's sight;
The moonbeam of his tranquil sea,
His one abiding memory;

For many moons her sister threw
Fresh brightness o'er her heaven of blue.
But plaided Scot soon stole away
The blushing star of life's young day;
Nor paint we now the parting hour,—
Those who have felt its depth and power
Would willingly the tale forego;
'Tis part of life—and life hath woe!
Nor turn we o'er another leaf,
It might be dashed with hues of grief;
Rather let memory's torch burn bright
For Ida, as she fades from sight.

## ON THE RUINS OF LLANTHONY ABBEY.

They stand, where the mountains around them rise
With crests deeply bathed in the azure skies,
Deep, deep in the heart of that lonely glen
Thickly shrouded away from the haunts of men,
While the scented sighs of the summer gale
Float softly along with a dirge-like wail.

Yes! beautiful still in thy time-worn dower,—
For ages have past, thou pale wintry flower:
But the hills around thee their vigil keep,
And the stars pour dreams on thy solemn sleep,
While the loving moon sends her glances through
Thy mouldering aisles, from her heaven of blue;
And the gray mournful lichen weaves its braid,
As the blast whistles through thy depths of shade,
And the clouds, their heavy lids fringed with dew,
Softly weep on thine emerald turf anew.

While thy dreamy river still murmurs on
A requiem faint to thy glory gone.

. . . . . .

Once in earlier time, a lone shrine was there,
Full dark and austere was that cell for prayer;
From king Arthur's court, saintly Dewi came
To burn on its altar life's quivering flame;
There to spend the eve of his priestly days
In fast and in vigil, in chaunt and praise;
Far, far from the tumult of war and strife,
Enwrapped in the raiment of hermit life;
From the chivalric deed, and the Knightly art
To commune for aye with his lonely heart;
Away from great Arthur whose wisdom shed
Grace o'er the rude tribes that owned him Head;
O'er tower, and hamlet, and forest green;—
But these are the shadows which once have been.

. . . . . .

For the Norman came, with his iron host,
And fast paled the pride of our rocky coast;
The Dane and Saxon, soon melted away,
As the mountain mist and the ocean spray,
For the Conqueror's host spread far and wide,
Like the mighty rush of the ocean tide;

And one of his noblest to Hondhu came
In search of high quarry and mountain game;
De Laci, who bravely at Hastings' fight
Drew his ready blade in the Norman's right;
Now boldly hunted the antlered deer
Through fell and through forest, thro' lake and mere,
Till wearied, he lay on a grassy mound
To drink in the beautiful depths around;
To feel with the pulse of another life,
That man was not born to live for strife.
So he stayed him long by that lonely cell
To ponder on deeds remembered well,
And feel that a home in that scene sublime
Might wean his soul from the things of time;
So straitly he nerved him to give up all,
And brace his proud heart in the hermit's thrall:
Thus the bold De Laci with falcon eye,
The mirror of knighthood—came there to die.

Ah! perchance life's struggle had never brought
The good his proud spirit had keenly sought;
Or perchance he felt, as we each should feel,
That all is but dross save the spirit's weal:
That the glitter of life like the morning dew,
Had faded away in time's long review—
And recluse at once in life, garb and fare

The stately De Laci bowed low in prayer,
Placed hair-cloth sere neath his armour bright,
Till the dews of heaven and chills of night
Slowly wasted those arms of proof away—
Ah! little he recked it on Hastings' day!

So Time's wave rolled on, and De Laci grew
In most saintly fame in the world's review;
When to his lone cell came in holy guise,
With bell and with book a grave chaplain wise;
And churchman and warrior builded a fane,
And nobles from far, both with might and main,
Poured gifts and gold like a flowing tide,
And a structure arose near the mountain side,
Like a dream in stone, or a beautiful thought,
As if Genii the magical deed had wrought.

Now Ruin laughs loud and decay has thrown
Her weir'd mourning mantle o'er fretted stone;
And o'er lichened arch and crumbling tower
Her pall hangs heavy in sun and shower;
Yet still, like a twilight from other years,
Like a gleam of gladness through sombre fears,
Like a voice from the past with subtle spell,
Thou breathes on our hearts thine own sad farewell.

. . . . . .
.

The blood of the Norman lies thickly there;
De Laci—who builded that house of prayer;
Noble Knights who wore well proud crest and shield;
The stout hearts of price that would never yield
Lie dreamless—each once in his narrow cell,
In glory—still guarded by potent spell:
While the moon for aye doth her vigil keep,
To silver the turf where the mighty sleep.

They rest in the shade of their mighty pile:
Hush! list to the dirge in that sainted aisle;
Be still—lest pale Shadows around thee creep;
Let no whisper disturb their dreamless sleep,
Lest thou start at the clank of an iron heel
Or unearthly flash from a casque of steel;
Lest the nave be thronged with the ghastly dead,
And thy blood fast curdle to sounds of dread;
Or through the lancet, sighs fall on thine ear
Chilling thy heart with the pale pulse of fear;
Or in fancy thou hear'st the tinkling bell
As Shade follows Shade to each narrow cell;
While the moaning wind their requiem sings,
And dim twilight saddens all earthly things.
But let Fancy picture the sweet sad chime
Which fell on the ear at the hour of prime;
As perchance some heart deeply swathed in grief

In those stately walls had sought calm relief;
Relief from an anguish that never slept;
But as years rolled on, still more closely crept,
Crept round the heart strings with chilling force,
Till the breathing form like a living corse
Coldly dreamed onwards, as though the soul
Had already past to the longed for goal.
Still the eye of pride and the stately mien
Shadowed forth the puissance that once had been,
Tho' the heart waxed still as if life were gone
And the living lips were nigh turned to stone.

Alas! for the sadness on which no ray
Of this beautiful world pours a living day.
Alas! for the spirits which cannot turn
From the far-off altars on which they burn;
Still burn the incense of other years,
And give to the present not even tears.
By whom prime and matins and evensong
Are unheard, while phantoms around them throng,
As the cloisters echo their measured tread,
While softly the dirige sounds for the dead.
Perhaps their sad thoughts rest on Holy Shrine,
When in happier days in fair Palestine
They buckled on armour against Paynim foe,
And in well-fought field laid the Moslem low.

Perhaps in some tilt on a sunlit plain
Where high deeds of prowess withouten stain,
Had won the fair guerdon of dauntless knight
With spurs buckled on by a Lady bright.

Alas! for the dreams that return again
When sleep has but lulled the anguish of pain;
And woe to the dreamer who wakes to the truth,
And feels he wakes not to the language of ruth:
To whom dull routine and the daily round
Of duty forsooth, is an empty sound.
Who have vainly sought in a monk's dull cell,
To shun some bright Pharos remembered well—
To forget the far beacons which lured them on—
Where, where is Nepenthe so rarely won?

But others there may be in sober guise,
Other hearts before whom the future lies
Not rayed with bright hues, but with even light
From a far horizon with sunset bright;
Which tells of the glory which yet may be,
Ever brighter still, as life's shadows flee
Before the deep calm, which in weary breast
Preludes to the heart its long wished for rest:
To these pilgrims, life's daily lesson brings
Fair symbols of peace on Time's vanishing wings.

Who shall sum the thoughts that awaken there?
I fear me that earth twines too close with prayer,
For sad sighs fall fast as the summer breeze
Comes laden with life from the forest trees;
When at twilight the stars beam dimly through
From their far off homes in the midnight blue,
While the moonbeams silver the cypress glade,
But alas they light not the heart's deep shade.

. . . . . .

Say hast thou ne'er marked a smouldering fire
From its dusky heap send forth jet of ire?
As through ashen mass a faint breath has crept,
Which might else in its dull repose have slept;
So stirred by a sound, a sigh, a token,
The shivered heart unites links long broken,
To break again when mem'ry's pulse of pain
Stamps its dark fiat on the aching brain—
Thus they wear on thro' life's long weary day,
Weaving dark shrouds to shrine their living clay;
But while their hearts are buried in the past,
Have one stern joy, that death must come at last.

. . . . . .

The Past has a language 'tis well to learn;
It breathes from the dust in each mouldering urn,—
Through the broken arch where the starlight beams
In the shadowy forms that visit our dreams;

In the whispers that oft on our spirits fall—
And what heart can fly from their magical thrall?
For our pulse feels true to the sleepers there,
And our souls are steeped in the hues of prayer
While the present hour is enfolded deep,
As the past springs up from its mighty sleep.
For the shadows of time brood thickly here,
In their own deep mystery cold and clear;
And the solemn warning still widely flings—
So fadeth the glory of earthly things!

## ALIANORE.

There she stood—in the might of her grief alone—
Without pulse of fear by the sculptured stone,
In the grey Abbey church in the cloister dim,
The fair Alianore breathed the holy hymn;

While the diamond drops in her starry eyes
Were treasured safe by the pitying skies—
And the sorrows which marred her right queenly look
Were fast written on High in a fadeless book.

She knelt close by a tomb which bore on its breast,
The proud figure of one who had gone to rest;
With his sword and his crest and effigies high,
And a name graven on it that may not die.

Cold and drear lay round her the loved and the dead,
With signs of their glory all thickly outspread;
There—she stood in the might of her grief profound,
With nought living nigh, save a fierce sable hound.

All close by, lay the pilgrims from Holy Shrine,
Who had dauntlessly sailed o'er the foaming brine;
Some were clad in the pomp of their knightly pride,
And some with escallop and staff by their side.

In their armour of proof they lay stilly here
With the chivalrous look and mien without fear
But stilled were the pulse and the nerve that could dare,
As all fearless she knelt and breathed forth her prayer.

The churchman in stole, and the knight in his mail,
Seemed gazing around as she chaunted her wail;
As she knelt in the dawning, the hound at her feet—
While fast on the roof dashed the rain and the sleet.

Thus day after day in the depth of her grief,
She came in her beauty to mourn for her chief;
And ever behind her, withouten a sound
Stood wakeful and watching that terrible hound.

. . . . . .

The brave Lord de Sudely was murdered in day,
And black Leo's fangs were imbrued in the clay
Of the wretch whose strong arm in fury he bared;
But swift was his steed and the life blood was spared.

From his castle right early De Sudely had sped,
While dew glittered gaily on forest and mead;
The brave knight unarmed, save with sword by his side
Rode gallantly by on his charger of pride.

The drawbridge he cleared, and fast bounded away
While morn was yet wrapped in its mantle of grey;
The orient sun had well coloured his cheek,
And ever his arm was the stay of the weak.

He had fought in the East, and the Lion-heart knew
The banner of Sudely as foremost it flew;
And paled the Chief of the Mountain with dread
When pressed the Crusaders his flag at their head.

And fast he sped home to claim Alianore,
His banner laid by, and the red crusade o'er;
And passed o'er the sea with his good lance in rest,
With her favour still firmly wreathed round his crest.

Then he left her a space to return on the day
When midst courtly pomp he might bear her away,
For Richard the Lion in state would be there
And fair Berengarea, pride of Navarre.

Fair Alianore at her orisons knelt
And the Chaplain led on as the Rubric he spelt;
Soon the missal was closed with a sigh and a tear
As she craved the weal of the brave cavalier:


When sudden the sound of affright met her ear,
A shriek from the gate where the warden stood near;
For Leo was there with his lion-like crest
And glared his red eyes like to spring from their rest.


Then straight she fled down as the dog in his wrath
With might of a giant, rushed fast on her path,
And quick as a thought her bright mantle he seized
And gently compelled her to go where he pleased.


But suddenly staid she like fair stricken deer
And glazed her dark eyes with the cold damp of fear;
For lo! on the greensward, all cold in his blood
Lay noble De Sudely, just hard by the wood.


A blade of Damascus, keen edged to his heart
At a moment unware caused the life blood to start,
And the red robe of Tyre alas! proved too true
Some fiend from the East his foul hands did imbrue

In the blood of the bravo—a knight without scathe,
The truest in heart, and the noblest in faith!
And sadly they bore him with masses and knoll
Away to the church where they laid him to dwell.


Then that vision of beauty soon faded away
As snow wreaths fast melt neath the sun's potent ray;
And never again on those pale lips a smile
E'er quivering played that lorn heart to beguile.


O'er the dial of life, o'er that Lily of pride
Fell shadows of gloom which for aye must abide;
A dark cloud of sorrow had swept o'er her youth,
And nought had she left but life's sadness and truth.


And ever again as she knelt by the shrine
Where slept in still glory the last of his line,
At matins or vespers still alway came there
As mute as a shadow, that dark hound of fear.


Many moons had passed o'er, and twice had the sun
Thro' circles of brightness his fleet career run;
Still in the cold cloister pale Alianore
All wistfully breathed the sad dirge o'er.

Her orisons paid she was gliding away
When suddenly sprang the fierce hound on his prey;
He sprang at the throat, and the red stream ran fast
And rushed in the pale priests with fright sore aghast;

Just nigh where the heart of De Sudely reposed
The hound and fell murderer furiously closed,
But justice was due—and the Paynim lay there,
His life ebbing fast, stung with rage and despair.

Once more from the East, with companion too true,
He stole back to gloat on the mischief anew;
The Assassin's fell chief had ordered the deed,
De Sudely had braved him, he vowed he should bleed.

O'er sea, and o'er land, he had tracked the career
Of that knight without scathe or shadow of fear,
And sent the dark Moslem whose cowardly blow
Pierced straight to the heart, thro' the back of his foe.

For this he had sullenly passed o'er the main
To gaze on the proof that De Sudely was slain;
And silent and stealthy he crept to the tomb
While morning lay wrapped in cold stillness and gloom.

Yet tho' vengeance had slept, awoke it at last,
The curtain of doom was let down on the past;
Not death in brave battle, with face to the foe
But a blood-hound's keen fangs laid the Saracen low.


And that mirror of fealty lay by his side,
For Sudely he lived, to avenge him he died;
And hearts which beat true must still lovingly throw
Pity's rays round the faith of long ages ago.

   .      .      .      .      .      .

The convent's cold walls shielded Alianore,—
'Twas but a short shrift and life's conflict was o'er;
So they laid her to rest in the cloister so dim,
By the side of De Sudely with ave and hymn:


While the grave priests stood by, with torch and with stole
To pray for the peace of the young sister's soul,
And the loved, and loving, laid chaplets so fair
O'er the heart in its cold rest, left mouldering there.

## IONA.

Iona, cradled on the deep,
The wild North seas around thee sweep,
Not thine the Southern rippling waves
That idly fret their coral caves
Whose clear deep waters softly driven,
Know not the rougher gales of heaven.
Not rising from a zone of blue,
Fair reflex of the heaven's own hue,
But belted by the sea-green wave,
The home of hearts both true and brave,
Which beat with hopes and pulses high
Beneath their own more cloudy sky;
Gorgeous and beautiful to view
When golden sunlight dazzles through,
Or softer moonbeams gently play
O'er the low hills that guard the bay.
How many centuries have swept
Since Columb, his lone vigil kept!
Since first he passed the stormy seas

That girdle round the Hebrides;
And looked his last on that fair Isle,
Where greenest meadows gaily smile
With tender dew drops glittering o'er,
Like diamonds set in emerald floor.

No more to hear the sounding swell
Of Island waves beloved so well,
In solemn cadence soft and low
Arousing thoughts of long ago:
Not calm as in life's earlier hours
Of April sunshine and sweet showers,
When light and gladness seemed to be
The heralds of futurity,
But clash of arms, and hasty mood
His better life had nigh subdued,
Left him to mourn o'er sudden wrath
Which flung such darkness on his path;
For ill his mighty heart could brook
Nor hasty word nor angry look;
His clear blue eyes' mild loving light
Would deepen fast at grief or slight;
But higher power and holy dream
Full soon St. Columb felt I deem,
And left the Isle of Saints to find
A home to calm his 'wildered mind;

To seek the peace he might not know
Amidst the scenes, where long ago
He wandered oft in sage dispute,
Till every other tongue was mute.

Columba's name in morning life
Was changed for one with meaning rife,
Sweet name of rest, "The Churches' Dove,"
Was given to image forth his love;
And schools the young Saint founded then
To spread the Gospel scheme to men—
Fair Daremagh, Kells, and those on Foyle,
Rose up with loving care and toil;
And for a thousand years the last
Had held his Saintly memory fast;
But chance, and change, and foreign rule
Have dimmed the legends of the school.
Yet at gray Kells may still remain
The last link of that broken chain,
The Oratory, where he taught
The sacred lore so keenly sought;
And where that bright illumined page
Mute marvel of such early age,
Was written by his careful hand
To guard grave truths by Wisdom planned;
Blazoned with colours, and encased

In silvery sheath all deftly traced,
And laid in Eardham of the Pile
Or safer still, in its fair aisle;
But once was rudely reft away
And hidden from the light of day,
To gain its gold at any cost:
Oh for this love, what souls are lost!
But after twice the moon passed through
On her high course, far realms of blue,
Again was in sweet bondage kept
Until at last it safely slept
In learned college—classic home,
Fit rest for such a priceless Tome.

Some said 'twas written at Moville
And was the cause of grievous ill,
That night and day the Saint worked there
On leaves so marvellously rare;
But Finian, potent at the school,
Pronounced the deed a breach of rule;
And thence sprang up dissension strong,
For Columb felt it grievous wrong:
Not his, the mighty heart to brook
The course fierce Dermot instant took;—
Dermot, proud sovereign of the Isle,
Ordered the transcript to Moville.

. . . . .

There was dismay in Tara's Halls,
And strife rose up in princely walls,
For Aidan's brave and gifted son
Was there as hostage, fairly won;
For at great Dermot's regal court,
Full many came in gay resort:
Tara, where Erin's royal race
Held pomp and sway with regal grace,
Ere Lorha's Saint his ban had thrown
O'er stately Rath and fretted stone,
And Ferran's mighty circle still
Rested zone like, around the hill,
And stood high Teamor's banquet hall
With its twelve gates along the wall—
I said strife rose—and Curnan slew
In hasty fight a noble true,
And to Daremagh for refuge came,
Daremagh—where Saint Columba's fame
Drew many hearts, this erring guest
Came in hot haste in search of rest;
And Columb sheltered him from death
In hope to win him to the Faith;
But the vexed king sent mighty force,
And the poor youth soon slept—a corse.

Such broken pledge of solemn oath,
Of knightly faith and kingly troth,
Columb's chafed spirit ill could bear;
And then loud rose the cry for war.
His slumbering, hasty mood brake forth,
And flying quickly to the North
He roused the Ulster princes then;
And their brave king and noble men
Decreed that Dermot, chief of all
The author of such deed, should fall.
But Erin's sovereign replied
By sending trusty men and tried,
To wreak on rebel vassal's woe
In great and speedy overthrow.

Then woke stern battle's mighty roar,
As beat the billows on the shore;
And on Cul-dreivne's fated plain
The warring chieftains fought amain,
Until proud Dermot's leaguering host
Fast paled away like winter frost;
And long he sadly rued the hour
When he vexed the Northern power;
For cold and ghastly on the field
Lay hearts of price that would not yield;
But Ulster's hardy sons fared well,

Perchance the cause were hard to tell;
Some said Columba's earnest prayer
Had not been lost upon the air,
And some,—but 'tis our lot to tell
Upon that field the mighty fell.

But soon as passion spent its force
Came thy keen pangs, O dire Remorse!
When the wild din of war was hushed,
And Columb's rivals deeply crushed,
Replaced beneath his sheltering care
The Volume, rich beyond compare:
Then woke the anguish of his soul,
For reason ruled with stern control;
And conscience with cool whisper, still
Would not be cancelled by the will:
And long he rued the hour of wrath
Which poured such deluge on his path,
Till Faith bridged o'er the wide abyss,
And Hope lit up Life's wilderness.

.   .   .   .   .

But when the Saintly Brethren met
With heavy hearts and sore regret,
That one so wise and good had lent
His powerful name to dire intent,

They paused, 'ere came the Churches' doom
Upon that deed of sin and gloom;
And fellowship awhile was riven—
Such the just mandate that was given,
For Holy Church might never wage
Nor strife nor war in that far age;
And sadly he transgressed the rule
The wise restriction of the school.

'Twas but a little space, and then
He entered the safe Fold again;
But still the stern command was laid
That he should leave green Daremagh's shade:
Stricken with sorrow, he complied,
And drifted on o'er waters wide.

So passed he from his Island home,
To breast the ocean's feathery foam;
Left Felim's royal home and halls,
And learnèd Bangor's sheltering walls;
Quitted for ever Diarmaigh
Which he had planned in life's young day;
" Green field of Oaks," as some may call
That long, long vanished convent hall:
And had not Aithne tears to weep,
Or were her blue eyes set in sleep?

Sleep, that waketh not to sorrow,
Night, that brings again no morrow?
Or did her son pour on her ear
The farewell tones she yet might hear?
What said he as the sun's first ray
Lit up the glory of the bay?
When came that sudden plash of oar,
And his last look on Erin's shore?
Though it is said, in after years
He once more mingled with his Peers;
But oh! how differently we view
Life's evening rays, which struggle through
It may be clouds which tell of night,
To morning gleams of golden light;
But that we know beyond the skies
The everlasting morn shall rise.

And twelve true brethren learned and wise,
Joined with him in his high emprise,
Full sternly trained in Finian's school
And taught in strict monastic rule:
Brendin's brave sons and Ernan too,
Tall Bresail, and the sage Fethoo,
The sons of Rodan of the hill,
And other names that linger still.
Some dear by kindred ties, and some
Who longed to lighten Pagan gloom;

Or it might be, the restless quest
For other scenes, in human breast;
Or hope to leave their cares behind,
Vain hope, as fleeting as the wind,
They still loom on, our way before
Until life's fitful course is o'er.

And once in his small bark afloat
Oh! who would trust so frail a boat?
From isle to isle his course he bent
Scarce knowing where, still on he went;
And paused on many a pleasant shore
In hope his stormy course was o'er;
But long as flashing eye could ken
The land he ne'er might see again;
The scenes he never could forget
And where his proud heart lingered yet
He dared not stay him, and the tide
Wafted him on o'er waters wide.
He knew fond thoughts might rise between
The present life, and what had been,
To mar, with old time memories now
The rigid life and weary brow.

Alas! how oft man's weary breast
Halts here and there in hope of rest;
And thus from isle to isle we steer

In search of good which dwells not here;
Some specious phantom lures us on,
And when we reach the bourne—'tis gone,
Like the mirage in desert sand
Which cheats the heart with hope of land,
Where pleasant springs may still renew
Life's withered hopes with healing dew;
Or floating Ignis Fatuus light
Which leads but deeper into night;
But Saint Columba's mighty heart
Had chosen now the better part,
Humbly to run the Heavenly race,
The Christian's path, with Christian grace.

And now at last he finds a rest
On bleak Iona's rugged crest,
Close bound by rosy granite rocks
Heaped stern and high in mighty blocks;
Where purple waters bathe the shore
Or lash the reefs with stormy roar,
And bright hues o'er the mountain, stream
With the rich glory of a dream.
There, scented thyme and clover green
And blushing heather grace the scene,
And hardy birds with arrowy flight
Glance to and fro like gleams of light.

Yet still an exile he must feel
When o'er his heart old memories steal,
For who can quench the love of home
When from its shores we widely roam?
And Columb felt he dared not stay
Where Erin's cliffs loomed far away;
His quenchless love of native clime
Died not—till he had done with time.

But still his chosen home was good
As he would feel in wiser mood,
When the deep shadows of his soul
Had yielded to a strict control.
So straight he nerved him for the race
He had to run, through helping grace,
To raise the standard of the Cross
On Pagan shores—all else was loss:
And letters teach with loving hand
That light might stream o'er distant land,
And the white banner of the Faith
Soon triumph over hell and Death.

Then careful works in convents grew
And learned life sprang up anew,
Since the long buried Roman time
When Genius set 'neath war and crime;

And fair the transcripts that were made
In lonely cells or cloister's shade,
And peerless leaves of truths sublime
Still live—weird memories of the time;
Dim light, from far Iona's shore,
Which long hath sunk to rise no more;
As in dark night, some loving star
Lends us faint glimmer from afar,
For sunlight can but scantly fall
On memories, shrouded by the pall
Which twice six centuries have thrown
Iona, round thy rocky zone,
Since first the wise Culdee laid there
His lowly cell for fast and prayer.

. . . . .

And rest we on the Abbot's knoll
Where oft he communed with his soul,
And keenly watched the distant sail
Striving full deftly with the gale;
Fair galleys, that from far and wide
Brought sojourners at frequent tide,
The friends his heart had loved in youth
Grave, earnest seekers after Truth;
And holy men from far and near
Came to hold converse with the Seer,

And passed o'er many a troubled sea
Safe in those convent halls to be.

From Ireland, and from Scotland came
And Norway far, grave Chiefs of fame;
And many too of lesser trust
Still hoped to mingle with the dust
Of Holy Isle—when life's short day
Had vanished like a cloud, away.

. . . . . .

There is a sleep upon the sea—
Its dark green waters seem to be
Instinct with some o'ershadowing power—
Dim spell, which stamps a fated hour.
A dull portentous silence reigns
O'er gray Iona's rocky plains;
And hush!—for passing o'er the main
Come those—who ne'er may come again;
Kings from the north, draw darkly nigh
In Death's last pomp, that they may lie
In Holy Isle—where waves shall keep
Stern watch and ward, to guard their sleep;
And Norse clad warriors steer their way
Till the dull galleys reach the bay:
All stiff and stark, their solemn freight,
But tenderly they lift the weight

And gently lay it on the shore,
Meet hymnal, the wild billows roar;
Nor other Wake is needed now
For said, the solemn dirge of woe—
Onwards, in mournful state they wind
With their dead burdens, safe enshrined,
To lay them in the Holy Place
In Reilig Odhrain, Rood of Grace.

How many Chiefs have rested there?
Dull pause—upon their stony bier,
In lonest trance, ere yet the deep
Cold grave, had closed upon their sleep.

O Reilig Odhrain! could mine eye
Pierce through the mists of days gone by,
Wind up the centuries that have swept
Since thine estate was trimly kept;
Oh! who might read the awful scroll
The long, long history of the soul?
Alas! we may not lift the shroud,
So look we dimly through the cloud
Just in the faintest light to see
The things which ne'er again may be
So gaze we at that rocky Isle
Where loving Zephyrs scantly smile,

For long, long years so widely blest
That Saintly Commune in the West.

. . . . . .

One morn, from Tor Abb's rocky height,
With waning power, and fading sight
Saint Columb blessed his Island home,
Presaging that in days to come
The great and good, would homage pour,
On cold Iona's sterile shore;
And many a fast and vigil keep
On her still bare and rocky steep.
Then wistfully he sought the Fane
Where sounded the long loved refrain,
The vigil of the octave done
His cell, with faltering steps he won,
Meeting old Luthan on the way
Who sought with patient mien the bay;
Gray Luthan, who for years had borne
From distant ground his freight of corn,
Bent down his head as if to weep—
Sad presage of his master's sleep.
Then Columb laid his weary head
On the stone pillow of his bed,
(Which wondrous stone, in later day
Long marked the spot where slept his clay,)
And with pale dying lips gave forth

Rules for the Brethren in the North,
Dear messages of peace and love,
Deep breathings of the " Churches' Dove ;"
The last faint efforts of that voice
Which long had made the Isles rejoice ;
That earnest story which will last
Till all the storms of life are past,
For love and peace will perfect be
When earth, and earthly shadows flee.
Then stayed his soul in silence, till
The Matin bell rang o'er the hill,
Rang forth to summon from their sleep,
The brethren to hold commune deep
Ere dawn had burst that Sabbath day—
Then rose he, hasting on to pray;
But when the faithful Dairmid came
And softly breathed his Master's name,
No words gave answer from the gloom,
The dusky church was still as doom,
For yet the lamps' unkindled light
Had shot no ray across the night;
There—close beneath the altar laid—
Slept Columb, in death's hovering shade.
Nature's last languor held him there,
Just moved the stiffening lips in prayer
And while around the brethren stood

He raised his eyes as if a flood
Of Holy light had passed between
The Life of Life, and what had been;
And with raised hand, his work now done
He signed the blessing—and was gone.

．　　．　　．　　．　　．

And twice six centuries have cast
Their shadows, since thy Abbot passed
Gray cold Iona—but e'en now
His name is graven on thy brow;
And long as thy bleak hills remain
It shall surround thee like a chain,
And links of stirring memories still
Encompass thee with subtle thrill.
Again with mystic eyes we see
In his dark robes the wise Culdee,
A man of such endowments rare
That few with him we might compare;
So noble his elastic frame,
So bright his eye with generous flame;
Or lit with scorn, or more subdued
With tenderness in melting mood,
Shewing the loving heart that drew
Around his home the tried and true,
Softening the cycle of those years
Besprent with many cares and fears.

The " Dove," sent forth to preach the Faith,
Ne'er flagged his wing till loving Death
Released him from the churches' care,
Which long with earnest toil he bare;
And so he loved and laboured on
Until the Victor's palm was won—
One sigh—and then he winged his way
For ever—to the Perfect Day.


## RODERIGO PONCE DE LEON.

Slumbers deeply Ponce de Leon—
   Finished now the long Crusade,
Never more shall Moorish Emir
   Of his prowess be afraid.

Slumbers he in his fair city—
   Seville proud in mourning lies,
Not a laurel leaf has withered
   On that brow of stern emprise.

Dreams he not of sword or cuirass
    Tossing plumes or helmet bright,
Dreams he not of war-horse champing
    Proudly eager for the fight.


Lists he not to stirring clarion
    Lists he not to tramp of steeds,
While the stirring blast of trumpet
    Summons to the Tilt of Reeds.


Never more his eye shall glisten
    When the beacon gilds the Tower,
Never more shall wild alarm-bell
    Summon him at midnight hour.


Lance and buckler hanging ready
    Ne'er again his hand shall clasp,
Ne'er again his war-worn standard
    Answer to his steady grasp.


Floats no more his noble pennon
    Over Moorish fortress high,
And no more the fierce Gomeres
    Rushing onwards fight and die.

Dreams he not, fair Andalusia
  Of thy scented citron bowers,
Dreams he not of swarthy Zegris
  Or Giralda's moonlit towers.


When upon its fretted turret
  Shone out far the vigil light,
Like the aspect of a planet
  On the loving brow of night.


Dreams he not of white pavilions
  Softly sleeping in the breeze,
When Castile's right regal banner
  Floated high midst scented trees.


Calls he not the Adelides
  As they march with stealthy tread,
Calls he not the Escaladors
  With De Prado at their head.


Dreams he not, fair Guadalquiver
  Of thy myrtle-scented banks,
When pressed on his heavy squadrons
  To attack El Zagal's ranks.

Graceful in the Tilt and Tournay,
  Mighty in his cuirass bright,
On Alhama's battlements
  Stood he firm to guard the right.

While far off the dark Sierras
  Slept still coldly in the morn,
Ere their stately cloud-capt summits
  Shone in lustre newly born.

Proudly trod his cuirassiers
  As they left the dark defiles,
Just as glorious summer morning
  Lit the world with radiant smiles.

While afar the glittering beacons
  Paled beneath the blushing light,
And the Moorish watch-fires faded
  From the Turret's rocky height.

. . . . .

Died he in full tide of glory,
  In the splendour of his might.
Ever at the post of danger
  Shone his crested morion bright.

Died he, ere his noble visage
  With the snows of age was crowned;
Died he, from the wear and warfare
  Which so closely girt him round.

Dress him in his costly raiment,
  In his doublet of brocade;
Wrap him well in richest velvet
  With his feet in crimson laid.

Place his sword so richly gilded
  Closely girded to his side,
So he wore it midst the mighty
  In his hours of pomp and pride.

Cast a pall of sable velvet,
  With a cross of shining white,
O'er the corse of Roderigo,
  O'er those eyes now sealed in night.

So he rests in his fair palace
  In the hall of lordly state,
There the mourners may surround him
  To deplore the good and great.

And when fall the evening shadows,
    Tell the Aves for the dead,
And go forth in sad procession
    With the bright stars overhead.


Oh! the bitter tide of sadness
    Deep'ning still the death-note swell!
Oh! the gloomy solemn cortège
    And the burden of that knell!


Twice a hundred tapers burning
    Shed a glory all around,
Glancing on the sable vestments
    As they slowly sweep the ground.


Now swell on the vasty concourse
    Bishop, priest, and friar old,
With the State's grave Guardians waiting
    On the heart, alas! so cold.


Banners ten bear high around him,
    Trophies won in Moorish fight,
Ere the stately Spanish Monarch
    Stirred him for the kingdom's right.

Stately walks the Intendanté
  With the Royal Standard high,
Stately, in the solemn twilight
  Seville's proudest chivalry.

Sad and sombre through the City
  Wind ye on, still moving slow,
Chaunting deep amidst the concourse
  Litanies in dirge-like flow.

Alas! for eyes, all dull and weary
  With the heavy tears that fell,
Knowing they might never look on
  The brave friend they loved so well.

Mourns he too, great Don Aguilar,
  Chosen of that mighty heart,
Friend and leader in the warfare
  Only death those chiefs could part.

Meet him, ere he reached the convent,
  Pallid Monks from sombre shade,
And with taper, cross, and censer
  Watch him in death's pomp arrayed.

Let him lie for state and vigil
    With the breath of sweet perfume,
Ere ye fold him with his kindred,
    Fold him to the house of gloom.


Then receive him midst the number
    Of the hearts that ache no more;
There no clarion shall arouse him,
    There life's weary watch is o'er.


Lift on high his hard-won banners—
    Banners ten—with heavy swell,
They will hang full cold and stately
    O'er the heart that loved them well.


So for ages lay he calmly,
    Those still pennons o'er his head,
Till fierce warfare grew around him
    And disturbed the mighty dead.


Overturning the fair marble
    Where high-hearted Leon slept,
Scattering wide a hero's honours
    Which three centuries had kept.

Oh! the anguish that lay heavy
   O'er the land of Spain that day,
When her Roderigo's ashes
   Were so rudely swept away!

But again they have been gathered—
   In the chapel where he slept,
One of his own mighty lineage
   Hath a loving vigil kept;

Graving near the antique altar
   Leon's knightly name so high,
Saying to the heart "Here resteth
   The mirror bright of Chivalry."

# NIGHT IN GRANADA.
## 1492.

There were lights upon the turrets,
  There was hurrying to and fro,
And the clanging of bright armour
  With stern menace to the foe;

And the champing of fleet horses
  With their desert eye of pride,
Their silky manes still tossing high
  And their nostrils open wide.

There were slingers and cross-bow men
  Fast arraying for the fight,
With ready scymetars unsheathed
  In the deep, deep hush of night.

There was buckling on of cuirass
  And fastening yataghan,
And the eager look of foemen
  As they hurried to the van.

Some their lances bore and targets,
  Some bore steely corslets bright,
Others in Damascened armour
  Were in costly fashion dight.


Then bright amulets were fastened
  With a missive from the Book,
And starry talismans to charm
  Dark Azrael's baleful look.


And there fell a moment's silence
  On the turban'd ranks around,
While their glossy arab chargers,
  All impatient pawed the ground.


Fast from mountain rifts they gathered,
  With their gorgeous weapons bright,
And swarthy faces smiled at death—
  In that watch by pale moonlight.


Shone it on their polished armour,
  As it silvered o'er the glen,
And set behind the rough Sierra,
  Bristling thick with armèd men.

Fading in a dream of beauty,
　　Touching light the citron trees,
With their balmy breath still heavy
　　On the sleeping midnight breeze.


Paled the moon, as though her lustre
　　Ill became such scene of strife,
Where the mortal coil must tighten
　　To the last extreme of life.


Blazed around the fierce alarm fires
　　Every crag and cliff aflame,
But o'er all the din and clangour
　　Trumpet-tongued rose Muza's name.


Still flashed signals on the mountains
　　Through the vigil hours of night,
Ere the sun rose on Bentomiz
　　In a blaze of golden light.


But came the changing of the watch
　　As the dawn was breaking fast,
While lurid smoke from dying fires
　　Still rolled heavy on the blast.

Floated Islam's sable standard
    Heavily before the van,
Wild echo rolled along the heights
    As far as eye could scan.


Thickly stood the haughty Zegris,
    Turban'd hosts in fierce array,
With their banners floating gaily
    To the opening eye of day.


And they hied them to the battle
    With light arquebuse and bow,
With mantelet and javelin
    And firm step to meet the foe.


Rushing onwards like a torrent
    That o'erleaps its craggy banks,
Rushing onwards to encounter
    Spain's defiant serried ranks.


Alas! it was a deadly carnage,
    Cross to Crescent, spear to spear,
But shivered soon lay Islam's banner,
    Slaughtered lay her bravest there.

Silent now the clanging cymbal,
    Silent now those hearts so proud;
Woe still woe, to thee Granada
    They have passed like summer cloud.


Then, ah then! fair Andalusia
    Set the crescent star to thee;
Never shall thy moons of glory
    Silver o'er thy bluest sea.


Never more shall Moslem warriors
    Through Cordova's valleys pour;
Never more our fierce Alfaquis
    Vaunt the valour of the Moor.

.    .    .    .    .

Sped along a lonely horseman,
    Quicker rode he than the blast;
Foam bespecked his arab courser
    As with lightning speed he passed.


Through the postern of the city
    Dashed he in with wonted pride,
Then he laid him on the pavement
    By his master's feet—and died.

Mute and mournful stood his rider
  As the people gathered there,
Then outspake an aged chieftain
  " Bring'st thou evil tidings here ? "


Bring these parched lips evil tidings ;
  Thick in gory ranks lie strown
Our best and bravest on the mountains,
  Gashed with wounds I come alone.


Perished too my noble arab,
  He has died to bring me here ;
Haste, bring forth another charger,
  I must run my course of fear.


Oh Zareda ! Oh Zareda !
  Weep these eyes salt tears for thee ;
Had I back those days of brightness
  When thy priceless limbs were free,


Thou shouldest bear me to the Desert
  Which of right to thee belongs,
Far away from Spanish thraldom
  Far away from Moorish wrongs.

Thence I bore thee like a nursling,
    Smoothing oft thy glossy mane,
And I leave thee—stiffening coldly
    In this now degraded Spain.


Dinted deep my polished armour
    Where the flinty missiles fell,
Haste ye, haste, with fleetest courser,
    I have other woes to tell.


Onwards—for there now remaineth
    Little space while I am free;
Bury deep my noble charger
    By the love ye bear to me.

  .    .    .    .    .

Gloomy looked the Vivarambla;
    Gloomily the people there,
With their faces to the Caaba
    Looked the language of despair.


Still the city held them bravely,
    Still upon its towers afar
Stood the true and dauntless Moslem
    With his flashing seymetar.

Right and left flew Muza's pennon
  O'er the gates and on the wall,
And around stood ready horsemen
  Waiting for the trumpet's call.


Said he, better far to sleep in
  Lonely grave beneath thy wall
Pride of Moorish hearts, Granada!
  So my death might stay thy fall.


Rather this than courtly palace,
  Rather this than change my faith,
Rather far would Aben Muza
  Seal his Islam creed in death.


Better seek the Alpuxarras
  Far away from Spanish pride,
There—the Moorish faith may linger
  In its own unsullied tide.


Far from cold and smooth evasion,
  Dark deceit and treacherous wile,
And the saintly garb that covers
  Hearts that love to seethe in guile.

P

He who paltered to the Spaniard
    Reaps the evil he has sown;
Weakest shadow of a Monarch
    Bow to him who fills thy throne.


Let the traitor win his guerdon,
    Sell for gold his fortress high,
Let him bear his riven banner—
    Rather far would Muza die.


In the Prophet's Book 'tis written,
    And we cannot bar our fate,
Long the wary Santon told us
    Lost would be this high estate.


But whatever our condition
    Still we share a common clay;
Mind still makes the gulf that parts us,
    Else were all as wise as they.


Yet he made one mighty effort,
    Tried he still but tried in vain;
Sluggish now the tide that bore him,
    Camped the Christian on the plain.

Shorn the glories of the Vega,
   Spanish spears pressed thickly on;
Pressed around thy walls, Granada,
   Till his latest hope was gone.


Fallen the Zegris in the conflict,
   Lie the fierce Gomerez strown;
In the valley on the mountain
   Moorish hearts sleep thickly sown.


Said he sets our star for ever
   And we merge into the night,
Oh! that e'er such mist and darkness
   Should have fallen on Muza's sight.


Pales the Crescent fast above us,
   Dark Ahriman brands the brow;
Sows with salt, our fields of glory,
   To your black tents Moslems now.


Kept we not thy words Alwaken,
   For our Muftis said 'twas vain;
Not the wisdom of the Caliphs
   Could win back our land again.

Speed, speed onward to the desert,
    Shines the sun of Allah there,
Though from Mosque no gray Muezzin
    Calls our Faithful sons to prayer.

Speed, speed onward to the Desert
    'Neath its brilliant cope of stars,
In its depth of silence may we
    Wrap the memory of these wars.

Balmy still is happy Yemen
    With its flowers and sweet perfume,
There, our wasted tribes may gather
    Far from this dark land of doom.

So he bowed his face to Mecca,
    Bowed he to the call for praise,
And the diamond on his turban
    Flashed far back the sunset rays,

Shining with a light refulgent
    Like a meteor glancing by,
An Iris stream of brilliant rays
    But it flashed not like his eye.

That eye with hues of starry night
   Lighted by the soul within,
Yet gleaming soft with loving light
   Who that charmèd smile could win.


And true his heart in weal and woe
   Till every tie was riven,
And soft as his own crescent moon
   In its bright balmy heaven.


Said he thou wilt wither, wither
   Oh Granada! long our boast;
Christians scorn our fretted temples,
   Fast they mar our Moorish coast.


Could I dream, dream on for ever,
   Still those dreams should picture thee,
Bridge wide o'er the gulf that parts us—
   Still in dreams I should be free.


Yes, in saddest thoughts we bless thee,
   Core of every Moorish heart,
'Twould be life could we redress thee,
   Keep thee, even as thou art.

By our rival factions ruined,
   By our jarring counsels slain,
By the weakness of our monarchs
   We have lost thee, goodly Spain!


Loxa, Ronda, and Illora!
   Faints my heart and pales my brow,
Fires my brain to see the Spaniard
   Lord it o'er your ramparts now.


Now Castile's usurping banner
   Floats upon our Crimson towers,
And the haughty pale faced Giaour
   Scoffs amidst our citron bowers.


Fairer than thy vale Damascus
   Our own Vega in its bloom,
Sweeter than the attar fragrance
   Its soft breath of rich perfume.


Crowd around me brilliant Phantoms
   Crowd they on my aching sight,
O'er me shines the moon of Rejeb,
   And I stand on Calpe's height.

Tarik ! in thy midnight vision
   When the prophet gave thee Spain,
From the banks of Guadalete
   To the snowy mountain chain,

Did no evil whisper tell thee
   Loosed would be the Moorish grasp,
After centuries of glory
   Shivered wide that brilliant clasp?

Pass before me wise Al Raschid
   And the stately Almamoum,
Abdul-azis and Almansor
   Glide they onwards through the gloom.

And the gentle Abdurrhamen,
   Noblest of his Omeyd race,
Pride and glory of Cordova—
   Moves he on with courtly grace.

Ever still when sorrow loometh,
   That dark dweller of the night;
Ever still will busy fancy
   Come uncalled with spectre might.

Alla Achbar! we have sinned,
   And our sun sets in its prime,—
None can ever thee resemble,
   Brightest mirror of all time.

   .    .    .    .

So he left thee, fair Granada,
   With a proud and broken heart,
Never in a bondsman's bosom
   Could that mighty pulse have part.

Spake he not, as on he hastened,
   Mounting fast his fiery steed;
Quickly passed he through the portal,
   Passèd on with wingèd speed,

Nor drew rein till shone the Xenil
   Rippling in its silver light;
There the Moorish warrior stayed him
   In his own proof-armour bright.

With lance in rest and visor fastened,
   Stood he there close locked in steel;
Stood he there to breathe his charger,
   White with foam his fleet Zercel.

Heavy foam upon his housings.
  But he little recked it now;
Shone his Zegris crest untarnished,
  Firm his haughty eye and brow.

Proudly stood he by the river,
  Proud in his dark hour of need,
As when first upon the Vega
  Flung he oft the light Jereed.

Said he, in the sandy desert
  Scenes of beauty charm the eyes,
And the weary traveller hastens
  Where the sweet enchantment lies.

Waving palms and greenest verdure,
  Clearest fountains lure him on;
But alas! 'tis all illusion,
  Soon these shady groves are gone.

Ever thus life's day-dreams vanish
  Close around its shadows deep;
Let them close, for Muza fears not,
  At the end there will be sleep.

Pondered he o'er bitter moments,
    Lone in prowess, seared in soul,
Wrecked his hopes—yet little deemed he
    Life lay throbbing 'gainst its goal.


Met him there ten Spanish lances,
    And they closed in mortal strife;
Fought he though the odds were fearful,
    Still disdaining proffered life.


Wounded too his noble arab,
    But he reared his silken crest,
And with one last mighty effort
    Bore his master to his rest.


Plunged he in the limpid Xenil,
    Steel-clad horse and rider brave,
And with fleet and loving murmur
    The river wrapped them in its wave.

## THE MISSAL.

She leant o'er the page of that golden Tome
   While rays from the parting sun
Fell soft through the Oriel's blushing pane,
   Ere his western bourne was won.


And his bright hues fell on her pallid face
   Shedding calmest glory there,
As her lips half parted held commune deep
   With those old time words of prayer.


For the lines were written in Miniscule
   With storied message of love—
Lessons of holy vigil and prayer,
   And the fadeless Home above.


On the vellum page in a panelled square
   In hues of glorious dye,
Were marvellous paintings from Holy Writ
   To shadow forth Calvary.

On the marge lay ivy leaves deftly caught
   And flowers from Iris riven,
And miniature blossoms so gaily wrought
   They looked dipt in tints of heaven.


The blue cover was seamed with golden thread
   In blazon of herald's lore;
The quarterings fair of her noble house—
   High deeds of the days of yore.


And her dove-like face wore a deeper glow
   As she dwelt on honors won,
While in strangest letters lay weirdly traced
   The story of deeds long done.


The quaint symbols she knew full well to read
   In their bossy glory spread,
They spoke to her heart of the olden time
   Like voice from the slumbering dead.


But gently she fastened the jewelled clasp
   Of that tome of olden days,
And all quickly wrapped in its broidered shroud
   The illumined Book of Praise.

For the Vesper bell lent its dreamy tones
    To float on the evening air,
So she wound up her lonely orisons,
    To join in the chaunt and prayer.

## ON A GLOBE OF GOLD FISHES IN A SICK ROOM.

·   ·   ·   ·   ·   ·

And I have made your crystal home
    As bright as home could be,
And graced it with the feathery moss
    And shell from the deep sea.

Your brightness shed on weary hours
    A magic and a balm,
Oft lending fever's lightning pulse
    The shadow of a calm.

And wistfully I gazed on you,
    When throbbing brow and brain
Could bear to look at little else
    In the dim halls of pain.

That day has past and perished too
   Those little gleams of light,
Which ofttimes in my darkened room
   Shed fitful lustre bright.


But unforgotten still those hours
   In which ye played a part,
When ye flung pale rays of sunshine
   On the shadows of my heart.


And memory weaves an Iris braid
   Of loving looks that threw
A halo o'er those suffering days,
   Still bright in long review.

# Songs of Home.

### TO F. F.

I was too happy ere this hour
   To borrow aid from song;
But absence from thee wakes the lyre
   Which now has slumbered long,
And makes me seek, as I have done
   Full oft in days gone by,
The dreamy charm, the soothingness,
   The spell of poetry.

And when amidst lonely watchings
   A step falls on my ear,
I look up anxious for the voice
   My heart so longs to hear,
Forgetting the white-crested waves
   That roll between us now,
And looking vainly for thy hand
   To smooth my fevered brow.

Our little babe upon my knee
    Looks up with laughing eyes;
Say, when will glisten those bright orbs
    With light of glad surprise,
To hear the voice she knows so well,
    And carolling in air,
Rejoice within her father's arms,
    Unconscious of his prayer!


Oh! 'tis a blessed thing to hear
    Those scarcely breathed words,
Which strike with such intensity
    Upon the heart's full chords;
Oh! 'tis a blessed thing to gaze
    Upon that little brow,
Ere time hath pierced the mine of thoughts
    Which lie asleep below!


The hours pass slowly by, dearest,
    Without thy sunny smile,
To brighten each hour of gladness,
    And every care beguile;
But thy love is ever round me,
    A safeguard and a spell,
An atmosphere of happiness
    In which I love to dwell.

Though the fire is burning brightly,
    Thou art not by our hearth,
Thou, who art dearer to this heart
    Than anything on earth;
And one sweet face looks gaily round
    Another form to see,
To talk to her of pretty things
    And dance her on his knee.

And when the day of rest draws nigh
    Thou art not by my side,
To make its hours of peacefulness
    With quickened footstep glide;
To look on the leaves which tell us
    We shall united be,
When time to elder time is gone,
    We to eternity.

Thou art wandering afar, dearest,
    But thou wilt look to Him,
To the Ear that cannot weary,
    The Eye that grows not dim;
May His Presence be around thee,
    And thou wilt safely come
Where love's watch-fire ever burning
    Shall light thee to thy home.

1834.

## TO S. M. F.

Light be thy slumbers, my own bonny bairn!
Thou hast yet the dreams of this earth to learn;
And oh! may the thoughts that expand thy brow
Still leave thee the light heart thou wearest now.

Yes, light be thy slumbers, my bright haired child,
With thy golden tresses that float so wild;
With thy rose-leaf cheek, and thy dark eye mild;
'Tis sunshine that prompts that carol of glee,
'Tis sunshine in all that belongs to thee.

Still sleep, fairest, sleep, thy mother is near,
On high there is One who will hear her prayer;
One who alone in His wisdom can tell
Thy price to the heart that loves thee so well.

Rest, sweet one, rest, 'tis thy mother who keeps
Unslumbering watch while her baby sleeps;
She joyfully waits till those lids unclose,
Those sunbeams break forth from their charm'd repose;

Till she hears the music that thrills her heart,
Oh! fairest, thou knows't not how dear thou art;
That the priceless dower of a mother's love,
Is thine in its freshness sent from above.

May He be near thee, a pillar and cloud,
A rainbow of hope nought earthly can shroud;
May thy young heart be His, then will there be
True sunshine in all belonging to thee.

1834.


## TO F. J. F.

My spirit hath rejoiced in song
    Over one sunny child,
And Theodore my bright eyed boy
    Hath heard his chant and smiled;
And should not then thy mother's heart
    Pour forth my Frank for thee,
Its full and overflowing love
    In its own minstrelsy.

How often do I gaze upon
   Those dark and deep set eyes,
And joy in the returning glance
   Thy young heart's love supplies;
And feel my quick pulse quicker throb
   To the lisped word's demands,
The thousand little offices
   They ask for at my hands.

Oh! what a call it is to seek
   For holy help to be,
All that we owe my precious one,
   In deed and word to thee;
That so thy beacon lights, my boy,
   May never lead astray,
But safely guide and cheer thee on
   With love's unfailing ray.

For thou art ever on my heart
   With an abiding power;
A sense of blessing in His love
   Who brought me to this hour;
Thou bear'st thy father's name, fair child,
   Oh! be like him—and then
Thy mother if she see that day,
   Will live her youth again.

And yet a name is thine which brings
   Over mine heart a host
Of many dear and pleasant thoughts
   I would were never lost;
Of one who once thy mother loved,
   Aye, long before her boy
Could call aloud upon her name
   And fill her heart with joy.

Oh! may the Highest's blessing rest
   Upon thine infant head,
My sunny child, and on thine heart
   The Christian graces shed;
May'st thou delight to work His will,
   And then our Frank will be
A guerdon for the boundless love
   Our hearts bestow on thee.

1836.

## TO T. F.

And thou, my own sweet cherished one,
    How many hopes and fears
Are gathered round the zone of love,
    That girds thy infant years;
And early in thy glowing morn
    A mother's hand would fling
The fairest flowers along thy path,
    To greet thine early spring!

Oh! 'tis a blessed thing, my boy,
    To press thee to my heart,
And feel the quick warm throb of thine,
    All guileless as thou art;
While the feelings whose deep language
    Can find no breath in words,
Run thrillingly intense along
    The spirit's viewless chords;

And often silently ascend
  To Him whose love and power
Hath made my spirit to rejoice
  In this most happy hour;
In the bright sunshine thus to bask
  Of the heart he gave to me,
And thankfully to gaze upon
  Our babies on my knee.

Oh! how much beauty glows around
  The steps of infancy,
When ev'ry action, ev'ry thought
  Is redolent with glee;
Or if a cloud a moment light,
  'Tis chased away so soon,
'Tis but the dewdrop on the flower,
  A moment's rain at noon!

My very thoughts at times are hushed
  As to inhale the mirth,
Which bears as yet upon its front
  So little taint of earth;
To watch the spirit's well-springs
  Still ready to gush o'er
With some Iris burst of pleasure
  From source unknown before.

Oh! long may your young hearts, my own,
    Be bright as they are now;
Without a care to cast a shade
    Upon each sunny brow;
And oh! may He whose mercy gave,
    Surround you with His power,
And bless your spirits with His love,
    Through every coming hour.

1836.

## TO P. A. F.

Thou'rt welcome to our home and hearts,
    Thou bonny little gem,
More precious than the purest pearl
    In regal diadem.
Thou'rt come to share the love that flows
    From fountain true and free,
A source by others deeply quaff'd,
    Nor less the store for thee.

I love to kiss thy soft cool cheek
   Where the first rose tint lies,
And watch the opening dawn of mind
   Within thy azure eyes;
I love to mark thy curved lips,
   Fast gathering into smiles,
While the sweet music of thy voice
   So oft this heart beguiles.

And fancy, borne on zephyr wings,
   Looks into future years,
As her gay pencil paints thy sky
   With all that bright appears;
While the spirit thoughts which sleep not
   Ascend for thee on high,
To Him who still delights to bless,
   Whose love is ever nigh.

How often do thy soft blue eyes
   Gaze upon empty air,
Almost as if their bright orbs saw
   Beings all good and fair;
And if—though not to mortal eyes—
   Intelligences be
Permitted to surround our path,
   May their wings circle thee.

And onward still—when reason's thine,
  Look steadily to Him
Whose Grace and Goodness give thee light
  Which nought on earth can dim;
Keep thine eye fixed upon the love
  Which purchased this for thee,
And may thy earthly lot, my child,
  Be a bright lot to thee.

1837.

## TO W. G. F.

Walter! the muse which oft in bygone hours
Has decked life's path by strewing it with flowers,
Now that thy mother but faint homage pays
Nor trims her shrine, is niggard of her lays:
Nor gives me power to shadow forth to thee,
In fitting words, the thoughts that wake so free;
The hopes that hover round thee, and the joy
That fills my heart when gazing on my boy.
Walter! thou knows't it not, thou can'st not feel
The love intense that watches o'er thy weal;

A light which doth not wane, which nought can dim,
A cloudless ray, which shines on earth from Him
Who knoweth all things, and hath given this power
To gild the gloom of many a shaded hour;
Which human nature still must feel and bear
In passing onward, though its course be fair.

Yes, love unclouded, save by love's own fears,
Sheds golden gleams upon thine early years,
And hope in lines of light oft gaily weaves
Bright visions for thee, on time's opening leaves;
While thy dark eye, where loving rays repose
In liquid lustre, still their soft light throws,
Feeding the flames which burn so bright for thee,
The lamps of love which light thine infancy.

And oft while gazing fondly on thy brow,
Thy mother muses as she pencils now;
Gently parts off the shining locks which hide
That brow of promise which may reach so wide,
When slumbering mind wakes up in power to scan
Earth's varied volume, and the heart of man;
And oh! may thine which beats so quickly now
In the first flush of life's infantile glow,
When steadier pulses guide life's current on,
Be straitly bent for an immortal crown.

Run for the prize, to gain which life is given,
And know faith's rainbow hath its rise in heaven;
Spanning time's mighty arch, it marks our way
Till earth's brief shadows melt in endless day.

1840.

## TO J. D. F.

On memory! what a ceaseless dream thou art,
Binding thy busy thoughts about the heart;
Recalling scenes whose feverish hour is past,
And noting others, which now fleet as fast:
How great thy power to call up things unseen,
Clothed in the garb in which they once have been;
Giving the dead the homage due to him,
That mental verdure which time cannot dim;
Thou can'st recall the lineaments which now
Support the wreath on an immortal brow;
Give to the eyes the liquid glance of love,
Or mind's chameleon changes which did move
The kindly heart within; can't give a breath
To words of love, which now are hushed in death;

Give back the look, the attitude, the tone,
The place, the very atmosphere that's gone.

Well ! 'tis a precious privilege to gaze
On thy sweet face, and think of other days,
Ere thou to me a boon intense wast given,
Ere he, whose name thou bears, awoke in heaven.
My treasured infant, if that wondrous will,
A mother's love, had force to save from ill ;
—Like to the fabled Talisman, whose power
Was a sure shield in every evil hour—
Then would thy steps a flow'ry pathway trace,
And thy life's lot be cloudless as thy face.
My own bright boy, with those soft beaming eyes ;
Oh ! what a world of love within them lies !
At least thy mother thinks so, and 'tis well,
Her heart returning what no words can tell.

Yet though on earth no Talisman be found,
Tho' this fair world must prove but pilgrim ground,
Yet parent's love should do the all it can
And wisely lead the infant to the man ;
Endeavour straitly to direct his soul
To life's true end, the spirit's crowning goal.
If thou through faith in Him who for us died,
Who when on earth called children to His side,

Struggle through nature's weakness to fulfil
The gentle pointings of His holy will;
Then wilt thou have a Talisman, whose ray
Hath power to chase life's darkest hues away;
And which will lead thee, when life's span is trod,
To fadeless pastures in the fold of God.

 1810.

## TO C. P. F.

Like the winged insect dancing on the beam,
Or the gay Halcyon bending o'er the stream.
Like to all things which tell of love and glee,
Of such thou art—and oh! how dear to me.

Like the bright thoughts in love's recesses found,
Or gay spring flowers which gladden all the ground;
Like glancing birds which warble melody,
Of such thou art—but oh! how dear to me.

Of such thou art—but when dire fever came
And sent its pulses quivering through thy frame;
Thy painted cheek was anguish to my sight,
And thy dark eye too eloquently bright.

Like arrows piercing to the fount of life
And yet like balm to heal the inward strife,
Were those most touching words, beyond thy years,
A lovely picture set with mother's tears.

It seemed that nature could not love thee more, but now
That health is stealing o'er thy placid brow
Love seems to clasp thee in a tighter zone,
And prayer ascends that thou art still my own.

Now like a sunbeam glancing gaily round
While thy light footsteps scarcely print the ground:
Like odors, wafted on the wavy breeze,
Or music stealing through the scented trees,
A sound of joy, a watchword of all glee,
A smile on life—art thou my babe to me.

## TO C. P. F.

Cold lay the snow on its emerald bed,
And the stately dark elm its boughs outspread,
All spangled with crystals so clear and bright,
They dazzled the eyes with their silvery light.

And the north wind blew a keen biting blast,
And over the landscape its gray veil cast;
And the weary birds on sad pinion flew,
As thick on the green sod the snow flakes grew.

But a kindly and graceful hand had placed
A refuge for them in the snowy waste—
For those gentle warblers of summer hours
Whose lives lay hid midst the trees and the flowers.

And a loving eye watched the fabric fair,
And the glancing wings that oft floated there,
While the ruffled pinion and drooping eye
Looked smoother and brighter as she passed by.

But the sun came out with loving breath,
And the branches glanced from their snowy sheath,
As the brilliant pageant fled fast away,
Like the hues of the heart in life's young day.

And a spell of beauty past o'er the scene,
As the glad earth put on its robe of green,
While on quivering wings the warblers past
To brighten the face of the wintry blast.

Glance hither and thither, ye beautiful things,
Brush off the white crystals with fluttering wings,
Float past on the sunbeams, and look as if care
Dared not to come nigh such bright gems as ye are.

LONDON:
Printed by Barclay and Fry,
68, Queen Street, E.C.

www.ingramcontent.com/pod-product-compliance
Lightning Source LLC
Chambersburg PA
CBHW032134230426
43672CB00011B/2335